SURVIVAL IN THE WILDERNESS

First published in 2019 by Notebook Publishing,
20-22 Wenlock Road, London, N1 7GU.

www.notebookpublishing.co

ISBN: 9780993589829

Copyright © Dr Somendra Ghose 2019.

The moral right of Dr Somendra Ghose to be identified as the author of this work has been asserted by him in accordance with the Copyright, Design and Patents Act, 1998.

All characters and events described in this publication, with the exception of those known within the public domain, are fictitious. Therefore, any resemblance to real persons, living or dead, is to be considered purely coincidental.

All rights reserved. No part of this publication may be reproduced, stored in or introduced into a retrieval system, or transmitted, in any form or by any means (electronic, mechanical, photocopying, recording or otherwise), without the prior written permission of the publisher, aforementioned. Any person who is believed to have carried out any unauthorised act in relation to this publication may consequently be liable to criminal prosecution and civil claims for damages.

A CIP catalogue record for this book is available from the British Library. Typeset by Notebook Publishing.

In memory of my late parents

PREFACE

In the modern world, violence is a part of our everyday life, and we have come to consciously accept this. Wherever we go, whatever we read and watch is full of violence. Nothing but violence. There are various classes of people in this world, the majority of which do not want violence. Only a slight minority seek to fulfil their desires by choosing the path of violence.

In this book, I have made an attempt to project the fact that animal similarly do not look for violence or strive to kill innocent herbivorous animals. They need to eat, drink and survive, or protect themselves from attackers. There is no other alternative but to kill other animals for their survival. Without question, surviving in the wilderness is a significant challenge, especially when living amongst many enemies.

In the tranquil land of Maasai Mara Park, animals feel they can live in peace and harmony, with their food supply coming from outside the park. They, too, become friendly to everybody.

This is an entirely imaginary story; there is no reality. Reading this story, it is my hope that nobody will feel insulted or that the message is aimed at them, although there are some lessons for the younger generations. This is nothing to do with Safari park authority, the Maasai people or the Kenyan government.

INTRODUCTION

Kenya is a beautiful country in Africa, situated on the world's equator. It boasts many reserve parks, rivers, lakes and waterfalls, as well as a large and heterogeneous species of animals, birds and reptiles. Across the animal kingdom, the 'big five' rule the park, namely the lions, leopards, elephants, rhinoceros and buffaloes. This work discusses the issues the animals in the wild experience, when facing both other animals and human beings.

I've always had a soft spot in my heart for world travel; I've wanted to see, with my own eyes, different cultures, and to observe the animal kingdom and their behaviour in the wilderness. As such, in October 2010, I visited Kenya and was able to tour the impressive Samburu national park and Maasai Mara Safari Park, Nyahururu, where famous Thompson's Waterfall is situated. I saw Mount Kenya and visited Naivasha, Narok. The Great Vally Rift is extended from north to south. Samburu Safari Park is situated 350km north-east of Nairobi, the capital of Kenya. Maasai Mara safari park is located 150km south-west of Nairobi, and is spread over a 1,500km square area. The people of Maasai inhabit an area close to the park. The beautiful Mara River flows through the park in Kenya and Tanzania, and from Rift Valley to Lake Victoria.

During the course of my expedition to Maasai Mara, I was fortunate enough to witness the animals of the wild in their natural habitat; playing the well-known children's game of Hide and Seek. However, in the safari world, this game can result in the brutal killing of one animal, with its carcass subsequently used to feed other animals. It is a game of survival played between carnivorous and herbivorous animals. The predatory animal targets the weak, as well as young cubs and pups, or those who have been separated from the pack, whilst the plant-eating animals of the land live in constant fear of attack. Both groups despise one another and view the other as the enemy. Survival in the wilderness is a huge challenge.

After returning from my visit to Kenya, I could not stop thinking about the lack of harmony between the animals and how this is reflected in the way we human beings behave, particularly in relation to the animal kingdom. We, like the animals in Maasai Mara, seek out opportunities to take advantage of those in weaker positions, regardless of the feeble excuses we provide as our own justification and rationale. Our ability to trust has been lessened, and we accordingly seem incapable of living in peace.

The message of this book is centred on highlighting the ease with which all of us could live together in unison, each of us enjoying tranquillity. The basic principle we have forgotten is: we need tolerance and to love thy neighbour.

Chapter 1:
The Animals' Meeting

One pleasant October sunny morning in Maasai Mara Reserved Park in Kenya, a dominant lion invited all the residences of Maasai Mara Safari park for an urgent meeting. The purpose for calling such a meeting was, as he put it, 'to discuss some serious issues facing the park and its habitation due to the visitors entering the park, disrupting the peace and tranquillity, polluting the environment, endangering the lives of all the residence, and disturbing everybody's sleep from early dawn'. The lion also stated that the other animals—both carnivorous and herbivorous—must surely be having similar problems.

He called the meeting to discuss with all the inhabitants of the park their views, and stated that, if the majority were to agree, they would seek to stop this and devise the most appropriate action. Some of the carnivorous animals were eager to determine why the lion had suddenly called a meeting, which had never before happened in the park. Some of the herbivorous animals were frightened, of course; what would the lion say at the meeting, they had wondered. They imagined danger would be waiting for them. That night, they had remained vigilant, awaiting an imminent attack from carnivorous animals. They could not sleep.

Various groups of animal had had discussions amongst themselves. Why had the lion called a meeting? Nobody seemed to be able to arrive at any motive.

Mr Lion sent the invitation to all the habitats of Maasai Mara Park, using the services of the eagle. Mr Lion called the eagle and explained about the message and asked him to spread his invitation across all residents of the park. The eagle could not say no to the lion's order. He considered it to be a 'request or an order', but he couldn't grasp it. Whatever it was, why did he have to obey a lion's order? He wasn't his servant! But then again, he thought it would be foolish of him to disobey the lion. After all, whenever he was hungry and unable to catch any prey—which was not a rare occurrence—the lion would leave him some food; and although it wasn't delicious, it was enough to quench his hunger. He knew very well that, if he was refuse to help and carry out the lion's order, he would then not be given a share of food and would remain hungry. And not only that, but somebody else would do the work to remain on friendly terms with the lion. The eagle decided it would be in everyone's best interest to be the lion's friend and accordingly obey the order. As such, he flew across the park, from one corner to the next, and spread the lion's message to all residents of Maasai Mara Park, asking that they attend the meeting the following day. It did not take long for the eagle to invite everyone as he sailed across the sky. Soon enough, the message had spread across the park, as quick and furious as a wild fire in the jungle. The animals were puzzled; nobody could imagine why the lion would call a meeting so suddenly. They all agreed: this had never before happened in the park.

The following day, at the River Mara, under the shadow of a large Umbrella Acacia tree, the meeting was held. It was midday, a time when a safari vehicle would only very rarely be seen traveling the park, which allowed the meeting to go on undisturbed. Of course, Mr Lion wanted to keep his mission secret, especially from the Safari Park Authority and the visiting tourists; he knew very well that if the Safari Park Authority were to know the fact that he was the mastermind, then he would either be caged and transported to the zoo for good, or sold to another country.

Importantly, the animals attended the meeting not because The King of the Jungle, Mr Lion, had told them to, but because of the combination of fear and curiosity about what was going on.

Mr Lion was known to have a strong attractive personality, which other animals accepted, and no other lion—or indeed any other ferocious carnivorous animal—dared to challenge him for leadership. Notwithstanding his strong personality, some lions and other carnivorous animals opposed him, but they did so in vain. He had everything needed in order to be a leader of any organisation.

Full of determination, Mr Lion stood on higher ground and addressed the meeting so that all animals, far and wide, could see him, and so that he could also see them. He had a look around and found himself surrounded by thousands of animals. He had never spoken to more than ten animals in one place in all his life, and now he was faced with thousands, all of whom had gathered to hear his speech. He scanned the crowd, from one corner of the park to another, and saw nothing but the colour of the many different animals, birds and reptiles. He was nervous; his legs trembled seeing such a great number of animals. They were all there because he had asked them to come. But nerves would have to wait: he was strong, and he was well aware of his strength. And so, at that very moment, he made a conscious effort to gather his thoughts and addressed the meeting. He suppressed his fear and welcomed all the animals, using a loud, clear voice.

'Dear friends, sisters and brothers of Maasai Mara,' he began, his loud voice echoing across the park. 'I have called you here to express my concern regarding the future of the safari park. Our privacy has been broken by the safari jeeps. I want to share with you my experiences and then invite you to discuss your views and take a definite decision on how we can stop the safari jeeps from coming into this beautiful land of ours. Being King of the Jungle, I consider it to be my duty to look after your welfare.'

His speech was immediately disrupted by many voices, mostly from the carnivorous animals, namely the cheetahs, leopards, hyena and wild cats, with such animals recognised as not accepting any other animal dominating the park or dictating to them. It was a free park, after all, and everybody wanted to remain free of any restrictions.

A large, angry-looking deep-spotted leopard said, 'You are self-proclaimed leader and king, but we do not accept you as our ruler nor as King of the Animals.' The leopard received support from all section of carnivorous animals, their roars and yaps echoing across the park. He continued, 'You must have a hidden agenda or family problems and be trying to divert your problem to the safari park authority. You want to dominate the park. We know what's going on here,' he spat. 'You have called us here to cover up your own domestic problems by blaming others. There has been some talk amongst the other animal that you want to prove to your wives and other females that you are strong and all-dominant...'

The lion's opening speech was halted for several minutes as the leopard continued. There was much shouting—mostly from the carnivorous animals. Some demanded to stop the meeting and asked others if they, too, would like to return home. The lion quickly understood his mistake and corrected his words immediately, stating, 'I am sorry, my friends. Please calm down. Please hush now. I had no intension of hurting your feelings by calling myself the King of the Animals. These are not my words but rather those of the humans. Further, I don't have any intention of being a leader or dominating this park, nor have I any intention to impress any female. Please listen to me carefully.

'What I wanted to say is that this beautiful, tranquil Maasai Mara Park, which we have all come to know and love, and which extends far and wide, spanning more than a 1,500km square area of fertile land, belongs to us. Our ancestors lived here before, and now we enjoy the land, and our next generation, it is hoped, will live her in the future for many years to come. As such, it is our duty to protect our interests and the interests of our future generations. You all know we work very hard to live, and sometimes we are injured or fall ill and need proper rest—at least fifteen hours a day.'

From time to time, he raised his right foreleg in the air, making a fist to prove himself to be a strong, dominant animal, positioning himself as their leader.

The lion continued his speech and said, 'Listening to the melodious voice of the birds, singing in the Acacia tree near my den, I go to sleep in the morning.' He also said, 'When I close my eyes and try to sleep, suddenly there is the roar of the safari jeeps, which disrupt my sleep. I am not scared of them watching me, but the noise of its engine does not allow me to achieve any slumber. They won't leave us in peace. They come one after another, and when they spot us, within no time at all, more and more cars gather to watch what my family are doing! God only knows where from they come! But how is this acceptable? Once my sleep is disturbed, it is very difficult for me to go back to sleep again. There is no hiding place for us! They search every corner of the park, seeking to locate us wherever we hide. I don't know what they come here for. Why disturb our peace? I have even gone so far as to change my den—notably a few times within the last six months—but still they find where I am living. Their car engines pollute this beautiful homeland of ours! Sometimes, I have had difficulties breathing because of the pollution created by those diesel cars. They are nothing but invasive intruders. Of course, I recognise that surely all of you must be having a similar problem.'

His speech was so powerful that every animal listened attentively. Once his speech was over, he asked, 'Dear friends, do you have anything to say?'

There were muttering, but nobody said anything to Mr Lion. At last, however, a gloomy, hungry-looking thin leopard opened his mouth and said, 'I must thank you for your concern regarding the future of the park. I appreciate your feelings and I fully agree with you and what you have said just now. I have faced similar problems with the safari jeeps. Perhaps you are aware: I am skilled in climbing tall trees. I live in the trees, I hide myself, I hide my food, all at the top of the tree away from any body's reach. But these intruders search every tree and locate where I am hiding, and my sleep is also disturbed—not only by the humans themselves but also by the safari jeeps' noise.' In a little while, he spoke again and said, 'The other day, I think it was last week, after a difficult and tiring hunt, I returned home empty-handed. I was hungry and exhausted, and so I fell asleep. When I was in a sound sleep, suddenly I was awakened by a loud noise. Again, the safari jeeps. At first, I thought some other animal was invading my den! Lay at the top of a tree, I turned my head to locate where the noise was coming from. I was lightheaded, dizzy, and lost my balance. I was about to fall from thirty feet high up in the tree. And I knew I would die if I did.

'Fortunately, however, there were some more branches at a lower level, and those branches saved me from falling hard onto the ground. I must thank those branches of the tree for saving my life.' He then went on to state, 'We should make some decisions today as to how we can stop them from coming to this beautiful land of ours. My family and I am with you, Mr Lion, and you have our full support for this good cause.'

Many carnivorous animals shouted at the top of their voice. 'You are right! You are right!'

Others echoed the leopard's speech. 'We also feel they are disturbing our peace, sleep and tranquillity. And they're scaring our prey!'

A slim-bodied cheetah made his own point. 'You must be aware cheetahs are the fastest running animal in the Maasai Mara park. Nobody can compete with us when it comes to chasing another animal. 'I can challenge anyone.' He continued with, 'My family life is ruined and at breaking point as a result of the safari jeeps' invasion. Our privacy has gone and pollution increased.' He further stated, 'Whenever I try to get closer to my wives, the safari jeeps are there to take photos of our private life. And we all feel the pollution created by the intruder is damaging our health.' He took a breath. 'My wives have been after me to do something to stop the safari jeeps from coming to the park. If my private life is so often disrupted by the intruders, I am sure one day my wives will find some other strong cheetah who can protect them. Then they will leave me alone and go with him. Sometimes, I feel like attacking them, but alone I wouldn't be able to achieve anything. They'd kill me. I can't climb trees like leopards, so we are more vulnerable. Sadly, our next generation is not as strong as we are. They cannot run faster than us, and I am sure, if this continues, they will be more vulnerable from other predators.

'I must thank you for coming forward to discuss this ordeal. We need to take action to save us and our homeland from invaders said,' concluded the cheetah.

The lion continued to listen. When the cheetah had finished his speech, he thanked him for sharing his story.

Although the corner of his eyes had been closed during the debate between the leopard and the cheetah, Mr Lion had nonetheless noticed a group of herbivorous animals had been listening to his speech from afar, their eyes watchful with the fear of being attacked by other animal. Mr Lion knew very well that he needed to win the hearts of the herbivores if he was to accomplish his mission; after all, they made up the majority of the safari park.

He addressed the herbivorous animals and said, 'Dear friends, why are you standing so far away? Come closer. We are all friends. As from today, you won't have to be scared of us. We will all be one big animal family and we will all be friends. Please come closer.' Mr Lion impressed the animals further when he said, 'I can assure you that no carnivorous animal will attack you when you attend any meeting. More so, two hours after the meeting has been declared closed, you can return safely to your home.'

A Thompson's gazelle, light-brown in colour with black stripes and long, pointed horns, looked on with both fascination and suspicion, his eyes watching all the carnivorous animals. He tapped his friend's head with his own, and took a bouncing leap before asking, 'My friend, do you believe this? They are crafty buggers. This is nothing but a trap for us. If we were to believe his words, very soon after we'd all be killed.'

The Thompson's gazelles, as grassland inhabitants, recognised their main predator as the cheetah. But they also recognised that they can run faster, at 80–96 kilometres, and can twist and turn at speed in an effort to save themselves from predators. They know it very well that cheetahs are short-distant runners and cannot chase them for more than a few hundred yards.'

A large number of gazelles then shouted at the lion. 'We are not coming closer into your trap! You are very cunning! We know you very well! You will betray us! You must have some kind of hidden agenda. If you stop hunting us for food, then what are you going to eat? Grass like us? Ridiculous!' This was said in a rather scathing tone. A burst of amused and cynical giggles erupted amongst the herbivorous animals. The gazelles looked around suspiciously, on the lookout for any impending danger of attacks from carnivorous animals. The carnivorous animals, on the other hand, stood there speechless, with some feeling insulted but only muttering 'Stop this abuse!' whilst the others kept quiet.

Everybody was suspicious; nobody knew exactly what was going on and what danger could possibly be hiding around the corner, waiting for them in the dry grasslands where the meeting had been held.

One aggressive wildebeest said, 'We feel vulnerable if the safari cars are not here. They are our friends and they would never harm us. Why should we stop them from coming here suddenly, just because you are having a problem with your precious sleep? We don't see any problem with them coming here. They are not our enemy.' The wildebeest was afforded a cheer of support from the herbivorous animals.

The lion then responded, 'The purpose of this meeting is to stop the safari jeeps from coming to the park. This has been suggested in an effort to preserve the tranquillity in the park, to prevent pollution, whilst also protecting our own health and wellbeing. You must be wondering how this could ever be possible, but it *is* possible. You only need to trust me and cooperate with me.'

There was a murmur of disbelief and questioning as the crowd listened intently.

'I have a plan,' the lion continued. 'We would like to live as friends and not as foe. If we are successful in our mission, we will not kill any animal for living in this 'park.'

Zebras are recognised as nasty, temperamental animals if anyone is to get too close. They have got stripes—black and white; those stripes are like human fingerprints, meaning each animal's stripes are different.

One Mr Zebra said in surprise, 'It is beyond my imagination that, suddenly, carnivorous animals have changed their diet. Our flesh is no longer delicious to them, it would seem. You attacked us in a group and in a well-planned manner by isolating the weak, the infirm, children, and those friends of ours that had become separated from their group. You killed us in a reckless manner. You love brutality, Mr Lion. All of your pack does. How can we believe that, suddenly, you have become pious, honest and herbivorous? It would be unbelievable to take such a thing at face value. You are merely trying to deceive us with your compassionate lecture and I demand you say as much honestly! We may not be as intelligent as you, Sir, but we are not foolish enough to understand your motive, and so I ask you—no, I demand of you: don't make a fool of us!'

At this point, a sad and bereaved impala said took over the spotlight. 'You big liar!' he ranted. 'You killed my father yesterday!' His voice went dim and scattered. 'My dad was thirsty and only went to drink water from the river. He was trapped from the water by a crocodile, with you on the bank of the river Mara. At this very moment, the horrible scene still plays out in my head, in front of my very eyes. My mother, myself and our other relatives cried for help but nobody came forward. He was alone and helpless. Look at my mother. She is still in shock and has stopped eating, is speechless, and completely broken hearted. She is in a wreck.' The impala's voice softened and tears overflowed from his eyes.

Hearing the heart-rending sorrow of the impala's speech, a total silence descended, lasting for about a minute. Even the wind blowing a rustling noise of leaves could not be heard. The pleasant afternoon's atmosphere suddenly turned agonisingly cold. As if the whole Maasai Mara Park observed a minute's silence in respect of the departed soul of the impala.

Once the Impala had stopped speaking and the silence lifted, Mr Lion said, 'My deepest sympathy to you and your family. I didn't kill your dad yesterday, nor did any of my family members kill your dad. I have killed no animal in the last week. You have made a mistake. It was not me. It pays to mention at this point that we all do all look alike.' Mr Lion continued his speech and said to the other carnivorous animals, 'Look at the bereaved impala family. Don't you feel it is unjust to subject innocent animals to such cruelty? My intention to call you here is centred on the need to discuss with you how we can stop such incidents from happening in this park in the future. Soon, we have to stop cruelty to the herbivorous animas. They have got a right to live in this park with us. It is good for our animal society. I am fighting for everyone's benefit! The herbivorous animals are also animals just like us, and they have got the same right to live like any other animal—just like we do.

'Now don't misunderstand me! My intention is honest and straight-forward. I hate killing the innocent, helpless animals for fun, but I have no power at present to stop killing animals to allow me to live. I am going to stop this happening in the park soon, but I would need your help, cooperation and full support.'

A big applaud erupted from all sections of the crowd. 'Are you prepared to bring this change?' someone asked aloud. Voices echoed all over the park; shouts coming from all residents of the park. 'Yes! Yes!'

Mr Lion then said, 'Be on my side and I can promise you, one day, we will win to make Maasai Mara a dreamland again.' The lion was given a huge applause from all the animals.

'How it this even possible?' the dik dik (smallest antelope) asked in concern.

Mr Lion replied, 'It is possible if we all are unite together and trust one another.'

The herbivorous animals were impressed upon hearing the lion's speech. Their confidence in the lion increased immensely, and they started to trust him, considering him a friend and leader. They all shouted, 'We have full trust in you and we fully support you!' Thus, Mr Lion slowly conquered the hearts of the herbivorous animals.

Still, however, he had a long way to go, and any silly mistakes or loose words could ruin his dream. This he recognised.

One very strong and young leopard then said, 'It is not that we always kill them. Sometimes they kill *us*!' He said this with a steely eye.

'Well then!' Mr Lion continued, 'ask yourself this: do they come to your den to kill you or do they chase you to kill you for food or for fun?'

The leopard replied, 'No! They wouldn't dare to come to *my* den! They know very well that if they come near me, they won't be leaving alive.

And anyway, they are scared of us. They always keep distance from me.

(Photograph by Ashwika Kapur)

In order to establish a good relationship with the herbivorous animals, Mr Lion said, 'You attacked them and now they have got to protect themselves. You know very well that they have got very sharp weapons—their horns. God has given them these tools to protect themselves, and you might get killed if a horn was to pierce your body during an attack. There is nothing wrong with this.'

The leopard felt insulted but kept quiet.

A cheetah then commented, stating, 'We don't kill them for fun but to allow us to live! It's survival! To survive in this wilderness, we have to kill. I don't like killing other innocent animals, but what can be done? We cannot live eating vegetables. There is no other alternative for us! If you have any alternative solution, feel free to let us know!' He then went on to say, 'Sometimes, we fight amongst ourselves for our 'territory, and that is also necessary to protect our family. We do not do this with other innocent animals.'

Mr Lion asked, 'If we carnivorous animals were to get our food from outside the park, are you then going to kill any innocent animals?' In one resounding voice everybody shouted 'No! Never! It wouldn't be necessary!'

A lioness was sat in the front row where most of the carnivorous animals were sitting. She said, 'I have got four calves and I don't mind anybody watching me from a distance, but I would not like anybody to come closer to my little ones. I feel insecure and like they are vulnerable. I wouldn't hesitate to attack them if they were a threat.'

There were many other mothers siting and listening to the arguments. Everybody shouted, 'We also feel our babies are not safe! I would not hesitate to attack anybody if I feel their lives are in danger!' This strong parental instinct was apparent amongst many of the animals.

One large, aggressive herbivorous animal, a Roan antelope known as Korongo, said, 'Now you have raised a very interesting point. Ask yourself: how precious are your babies' lives to you? We herbivorous animals also feel same way. Parents' instinct is to protect offspring from any danger by sacrificing one's own life if necessary. If you feel this way about your babies then why don't you think about our babies?' A large sound of applause echoed amongst the herbivorous animals.

Mr Lion said, 'It is very interesting to listen to your feelings about each other. But until we get our food supplied from Safari Park Authority, I have no power to ask you to stop killing other innocent animals if you need to do so to live. If any animal kills another animal for the protection of their territory, I also have no power to stop them.'

Mr Lion quickly realised that, alone, he was not going to win the hearts of the other animals. He needed support from all of them, and so he whispered in the ear of an elephant, and asked him to explain the purpose of the meeting. 'Perhaps they will trust you more than a carnivorous animal like me,' he suggested. 'You could convince them of the purpose of the meeting.'

The elephant nodded. 'Dear friends,' he began, 'I can assure you that there is no hidden agenda behind Mr Lion's proposal or in his mind. I have known him personally for a good few years—he has been my neighbour. He is honest, caring and sincere, and he wants to protect all the creatures living in this park. He talked to me regarding his excellent idea a few days ago, when we met in the afternoon whilst exercising. Perhaps you are aware, but I am not a carnivorous animal. Rhino are also not carnivorous, and we are not bothered about who comes to watch us. But nonetheless, I am still attending this meeting because I think it is important to listen to what Mr Lion has to say.'

The lion nodded in gratitude.

'Moreover,' the elephant continued, 'we are here to protect you! You should not feel that you are more vulnerable if safari jeeps were to stop coming to this park. I can tell you that they can't protect you and they do not come here to protect you. They simply enjoy watching one animal chasing another, they record videos and show them to others to achieve some degree of honour.'

A dark-coloured, large and very strong, but nonetheless beautiful, wildebeest said, 'Mr Elephant! You are the largest and strongest animal in the park. Your strength is no match for a lion's strength, but still the lion doesn't hesitate to attack you. You are falling into his trap, saying that you believe him. I'm sorry but it's clear that what he's talking about is rubbish!' He concluded his remarks in a loud and angry voice. He asked the other animals, not to trust 'these two birds of a feather.'

The elephant became very angry but quelled his anger and carefully tackled the situation. He lifted his head and looked around, careful not to express his anger. Instead, he politely replied, 'Dear friends, we are not birds of a feather. Mr Lion is a carnivorous animal whilst I am herbivorous. We are not the same. We are friends, and we want to change society. We can only do this with your support—with everybody's support! We do not want to kill any animal. Rather, we want everybody to live in peace in this beautiful park.' He then went on to say, 'What has happened in the past is not going to happen in the future. The world is changing quickly and we need to move with the times. I am sure Mr Lion is not going to betray us. If I feel any carnivorous animals are trying to play a trick then I can promise you this: all the herbivorous animals will unite under my leadership and we will drive all the carnivorous animals out of this park! So, for your information, I am telling you: we are the majority in the park.' A loud applause erupted. 'The herbivorous animals are the majority,' he continued, 'and so we should not be scared of them! Carnivorous animals know very well that if we were to unite, we could drive them out of this park! I am sure they would not dare think about that!'

When the cheer died down, a meek voice sounded in the crowd. 'But, if we are attacked by other animals and were killed or critically injured, what would you do?'

Mr Lion replied, looking around at the other carnivorous animals' reactions. 'The criminal will be punished severely and, in future, any other animal will have to rethink before committing such a crime. I must warn you: the consequences of crime will be a very severe punishment. Please tell your friends and relatives not to commit any such crime. There is no need for this. Any dispute can be resolved peacefully through the use of a mediator.'

Again he was asked, 'How will you find the criminal or catch him? No carnivorous animal will come forward and complain against any another carnivorous animal. And how can we provide the right evidence you'd need to punish the offender?'

The lion replied: 'We would hunt him down wherever the criminal hides, using everybody's help. Obviously we would require witnesses. The more witnesses, the better and easier it would be to punish the offender.'

There was some discussion, before the lion concluded, frowning, 'If we all get regular food from the park authority, then carnivorous animals would have no need to attack other animals.'

At one corner of the park, a large animal, referred to as Nyati, was listening to the debate. She looked around her with suspicious eyes, considering asking something, but shyness overtook. Finally, she opened her mouth and asked, 'Mr President, whatever you have said is built on correct insight, but, practically, it is very difficult to implement…'

'You are right that it would be difficult, but not impossible. Not if we all united together,' said Mr Lion. He chuckled and continued his speech. 'This is our first meeting, and I am very pleased seeing you here in large number. We need to continue step-by-step, and there needs to be proper discussion. Everybody will get a chance to put their own views to the audience. But what you need to do today is to decide whether we should go forward to stop the safari cars from coming onto our land. If we demand that the safari jeeps do not enter the park, I then cannot demand free food from the Safari Park Authority. On the other hand, if we allow the jeeps to enter the park, we can surely then demand food from the authority.'

After much discussion and arguments that went on for three hours, it all fell down to the majority decision: the safari jeeps should not be allowed to enter the land unless food was being supplied by the park's authority. Some became impatient to know the resolution right from the start, but Mr Lion replied with the need to follow the proper channels in order to ensure the success of their mission.

The lion had been expecting the worst opposition and was not completely optimistic that his plan would be accepted by all of the animal populations. He also expected that it could be very difficult to convince other animals that there was no hidden agenda underpinning his plan, which was a fear further augmented considering the opposition from various parties across the animal society. However, once the decision had been made by the majority, Mr Lion was extremely pleased with himself. He was relieved to have received the thumps-up from various groups for the big mission.

He lifted his right foreleg and thanked everyone. He said, 'Friends! I have no words. I don't know how to thank you. I must say to you that you have taken a brave decision to stop the safari jeep from coming into this beautiful land of ours in future unless we are given food from the Park Authority. I'm satisfied this is the right thing and that, with your help, we will get our food supply from the authority and stop any animals from feeling the need to kill others in this park.'

'Now, we will meet here again tomorrow at the same time to discuss our next step. Please remember that we will need to implement a number of actions: firstly, an association, which we should discuss thoroughly; secondly, the name of our association; and third, devise an action plan with attention directed towards what we are going to do and how we plan to do it.

'Each and every one of you, you must think on an appropriate name for the organisation, of whom you would like to be in the committee, and what action you would like to take. Do this before attending the meeting tomorrow.

'Now, I declare the meeting closed. Please inform any of your friends and relatives who may could not attend the meeting today about today's discussion and decision, and ask them to come to tomorrow's meeting. It is imperative we are all informed and on the same page. And, as I mentioned earlier, you have two hours to go back to your home before any animal attacks you.'

On the way home, the herbivorous animals discussed whether or not the action plan was the right decision for them and whether they were being naïve in trusting the lion and the elephant, or whether they were allowing themselves to drift onto the path of destruction.

In response, Nyumbu said, 'Let's see what happens at tomorrow's meeting. We can withdraw our support in the future if we feel it is necessary.'

The wildebeest also discussed amongst themselves. 'We are the largest group of animals in the park. Why not form our own organisation to dominate the park? If our voice is not heard, we might migrate across the border to Serengeti Park in Tanzania,' one of them suggested. 'My relatives live there and are happy to accommodate us in their country. So why not let's see what happens tomorrow.'

'You know what?' one wildebeest asked whilst grazing in the grassland. 'I wouldn't like to go to another country and settle there. We go for a few months every year. That's a holiday and it's different, but they might not like all of us settling there. There could be a food shortage or fighting amongst ourselves...'

'Well,' his friend replied, 'this whole world belongs to us. I will go and live wherever I feel I have got enough to eat and live in peace! I hate fighting! I want to see everybody happy.'

The day had been long and stressful for Mr Lion. He realised when reflecting on the day's meeting that he was in need of good support from every corner of the animal society if his dream was to transform from being just that to reality. He also knew that any loose words had the potential to ruin his dream.

After the meeting was over, the lion asked some of his strong supporters to remain behind for a few more minutes to discuss the next day's meeting. He explained his future plan to the elephant, cheetah, rhino, gazelle, wild cats and a few other strong supporters, and discussed how they would get food without killing any other animals. He asked them to attend the next day's meeting early so that he could have a further discussion with them before the meeting was due to start.

The day's meeting had given the lion immense satisfaction but, at the same time, additional worry. He wishes his friends goodbye before hurriedly climbing down from the higher ground and setting towards home. On the way, all of a sudden, he met a lioness who had been his friend many years ago. She told him, 'I am proud of you. What you are doing for us is our fundamental right.' She then went on to have a long discussion with him. 'You have my full support,' she told him.

Happily, he returned home. He sat in his den and watched the sun set, which he watched many times before. Today, however, the sunset was so beautiful, and he enjoyed it so much more than ever before, thinking about the next day's new and brighter, more colourful dawn that would be awaiting everybody The Maasai Mara Safari Park.

As the night time came, there was nothing much to do. Mr Lion thought of nothing but the meeting; he slept very little and could only think about the events set to unfold. The night was long. He was busy thinking about tomorrow and preparing his speech. He thought of a few names that might be appropriate for the organisation. He also thought that he would definitely need help from the Maasai people.

Chapter 2:
Sunset in the Safari Park

The following day, the meeting started at 12 noon, according to the plan. All the safari jeeps had left the park. The authority and travellers were completely unaware as to the activities that were going on in the park.

As per the previous day, Mr Lion stood on a higher ground, allowing him to see far and wide, just like during the previous meeting.

Talk of the previous day's meeting had spread across the park, increasing the number of animals that were attending to listen to what Mr Lion had to say. There were more birds in the trees than leaves.

Mr Lion was nervous; but nonetheless, he was proud at how he had addressed the general public in the previous meeting; using his loud and authoritative voice.

The elephant and rhinoceros, along with a few of the other animals, were his strong supporter and stood close to him.

'Dear friends, sisters, and brothers of the Maasai Mara Safari Park. I welcome you here for this meeting on this beautiful afternoon. I am very pleased to see you in a large number today. Please come closer. Don't be scared of any body. We have many important matters to discuss.

'Our first objective is to form an association, then to name the association and subsequently form a committee.

'In our previous meeting yesterday, you took the brave decision to stop the safari cars from coming onto this beautiful home land of ours, The Maasai Mara Park, unless our food is being supplied by the Safari Park Authority. This will help to ensure there is no need to kill any innocent, harmless animals.'

The whole park burst into applause, which lasted for a good few minutes. Once the applause had stopped, the lion smiled weakly and said, 'Yesterday I asked you to think of some names for our organisation. Is there anybody that wants to propose a name? Please come forward if you do.'

An old, infirm leopard slowly approached where the lion stood, pushing all other animals behind. Everybody thought the leopard had thought of an appropriate name for the organisation and would like to disclose it to the lion.

For a few seconds, everybody fell quiet. The leopard slowly climbed up the hill, notably with great difficulty, before getting very close to the lion. He then stretched his front paws towards the lion and said, 'My son, you are great. You are doing a wonderful job.

'Look at me. I am old, unwell, and cannot hunt. I remain hungry most of the days, unable to climb trees. There is nobody to look after me. I'm not alone in this state. There are many animals like me; dying of hunger. I will die very soon as a result of starvation. If we get food from the Safari Park Authority, I will then live for a few more days and will die peacefully. A hunger-free death is what I want. I have a family, but everybody is busy looking after their own. They have no time to think about their parents or relatives. They don't think that very soon they are going to grow old, like me, and need support from their sons, daughters, relatives, friends and neighbours. They have abandoned me. I am sure there are many more animals in this position.

'All my good wishes are with you. I am confident victory will be ours.'

There was a big cheer.

Hearing the painful speech of the leopard, a tear flowed from Mr Lion's eyes.

There was total silence in the park. Many carnivorous and herbivorous animals were also unable to hold their tears. Mr Lion asked the leopard to sit where he was and take rest.

'This leopard's speech has touched my heart,' Mr Lion stated. 'We must try to get our mission fulfilled. I will request you to please look after your parents, your brothers, you sisters, relatives and neighbours, especially if you see them struggling and unable to look after themselves. Look out for those who need help. Do not abandon them because they cannot look after themselves. Tomorrow you, too, will be old and unhealthy, and you would hope to expect good treatment from your family members and neighbours.'

Time passed by, but no appropriate name for the organisation was proposed by anybody. Each group of animals was seen to be talking amongst themselves, and the meeting seemed not to be making any progress. The lion stopped individual members from talking and once again addressed the masses.

'Dear friends, a procedure needs to be followed. If you want to say something, you must address Mr President or Chairperson.'

A wild dog, Mr Mbwa, said, 'We do not have an elected president or chairperson.'

'At this present time,' Mr Lion continued, 'I am in the role of acting president or chairperson, at least until we have an elected president or chairperson. And remember: we need to find a name for our organisation and then we will have an election to form the office bearer or committee members.'

Half an hour passed, but still nobody suggested a name.

Mr Lion said finally, 'As you are unable to suggest a name, I will propose a few and you can then decide which one is most acceptable to you.'

There was a murmur of agreement.

'First,' he opened, 'there is the option of the Maasai Mara Animals Association. Secondly, the Maasai Mara Animals Society. Third, the Maasai Mara Animals Federation. And fourth, the Maasai Mara Animals Union.'

A spotted brown hyena asked, 'But we are not as intelligent as you. Could you please explain to us what is an association, union or federation?'

Somebody remarked, 'You are crafty!'

The hyena didn't understand the remark, and considered the comment to be a compliment. 'Thank you,' he responded.

The lion replied, 'The meaning of all of the above terms is a group of people—in our case, a group of animals—united together to work together towards a common cause.'

A colourful bird known as the Superb Starling stated, 'We are not animals. We are birds. So why the name Animals Association? It should be referred to as the Maasai Mara Birds and Animals Association.' He then went on to comment, 'Whatever name you adopt, we birds must be there.' A long discussion followed concerning whether or not the word 'birds' would be included in the association's name. The majority of the animals rejected the motion, recognising that it would be impossible to include every group of animal, bird and reptile in the association's title. The birds were not happy.

Superb Starling

A seventeen-feet long-necked giraffe with a tattooed body looked around and said, 'Mr President, can I suggested a name?'

'But of course,' Mr Lion responded. 'By all means, let us know your proposal.'

'I suggest it should be referred to as the Maasai Mara Safari Park Association.' He received much support from his community, and especially from other herbivorous animals.

Mr Elephant replied, 'It is a good suggestion, but this name is not appropriate. This organisation does not belong to the Maasai Mara Safari Park Authority. Moreover, the Maasai Mara Safari Park Authority might object to this name.'

Many animals were opposed to the name and so the proposal was rejected.

A crocodile then gave his input, stating, 'We do not fall under animals or birds. We are reptiles. Surely any reference to this as an animal association is not appropriate.' The lizards all showed support.

Mr Lion asked, 'Crocodile, what is your proposed name for the organisation?'

Mr Crocodile replied, 'I do feel it should be called the Mara River Association.'

Again, many arguments and discussions followed.

It became very apparent that the meeting was not progressing at all. In the end, Mr Elephant said, Mr Chairperson, I feel we are unnecessarily arguing amongst ourselves. 'Animal' is a broad term used by humans. It includes all the creature living on this planet who are not human. The humans think they are superior to all other creatures, and so they refer to every other creature as an animal. I feel we should accept the name of the Maasai Mara Animals' Association.'

The elephant's proposal was accepted by many groups of animal, namely the rhino, gazelle, hippopotamus, crocodile and some birds. This was viewed as being a more appropriate name and was therefore accepted by various communities of animal. Nobody could suggest any better name. As such, Mr Lion said, 'As there is no name being suggested that is better than Maasai Mara Animals' Association, this is now being accepted. In the future, should a better or more appropriate name be considered, we could then adopt that name.'

One of the leopards was very angry and ferocious. 'We should not neglect the feelings of the birds, reptiles and other creatures who do not consider themselves to be animals!'

Mr Lion replied, 'Just now, Mr Elephant explained to you that all the creatures of God, living on this planet, are known as animals. Even the humans refer to themselves as a 'social animal'. I see no reason to object to referring to everybody as an animal. Furthermore, the reptiles and birds have accepted this so why are you objecting? Do you have another name to suggest?'

The leopard felt insulted, but replied, 'No, Mr President. I have no name to propose.'

A colourful Miss Superb Starling started singing with her melodious voice as she sat perched atop an umbrella Acacia tree, drawing everybody's attention to her. It was difficult to locate where she was sitting in the tree. Pin-drop silence was observed when she was singing, and once her singing stopped, everybody applaud her.

She said, 'I feel the name should be the Animals and Singing Birds Association of Mara as we live beside the River Mara.' She smiled down at everyone before continuing. 'You should know, there are more than 350 species of my brothers and sisters, all living in this park. Our community is larger than the carnivorous animal community.'

Mr Lion responded and said, 'Just now, it has been decided that no name of any individual group of animals is to be used in the association name.'

Miss Pala Hala was busy eating straw alone but was nonetheless deeply attentive to the discussion, and particularly to what the lion was saying. She lifted her neck, looked around and said, 'Mr President, can I suggest a name?'

Mr Lion said, 'Yes, sure. Why not.'

Miss Pala Hala said, 'I suggest that the Maasai name be dropped from the association as they do not live in the park. I feel that the Mara River Association is a better name for our organisation.' Support could be heard from various groups of animal and bird, but it was not enough to have an impact on the lion or to change the name of the organisation.

Mr Lion thanked Miss Pala Hala for her suggestion before saying, 'The name Maasai must be included as it is important to include them in our organisation. In addition, the park we are living in is the Maasai Mara Safari Park. We could need their help in the future! If the Maasai name is not included, the Maasai Mara Safari Park Authority might not listen to our cause and the Maasai people might not be interested in joining us. Not to mention that, without Maasai's help, we would not be able to communicate with the Maasai Mara Safari Park Authority!' Mr Lion stressed the importance of the name and the recognition that it carried a great deal of meaning. 'First impressions are very important,' he said wisely. 'When we negotiate with the Maasai Mara Safari Park Authority, they need to have a good impression. We want them to be open when they receive our letter. And in that vein, we need to have our own letterhead pad and our own logo. The name of the organisation can be changed in the future if necessary. So, my friends, for the time being, we should accept the name the Maasai Mara Animals Association.

A rhino responded, 'We should not forget the place we are living is called Maasai Mara. Whatever name we choose, the Maasai Mara name should be included in the title.' He was pleased to see most of the animals were sympathetic to his comment rather than critical.

The lion said, 'We have had enough discussion now. The argument regarding the name of the organisation has been heard and there should now be no more consideration as to the name of the organisation. We should simply vote for the name. So I ask of you: those who agree that the name of our organisation should be Maasai Mara Animals Association, please raise your hands. The rhino counted the hands on one side whilst the cheetah counted the other side. To be fair and ensure impartial counting, the eagle was asked to count from the sky, with the lion recognising that the eagle is known for his very sharp eyes, which are four times sharper than a human's, allowing him to see a wider area from the sky and facilitating accurate counting from the sky. And of course, the number was too large for a single person to count.

'Okay, now that we have counted those in favour,' Mr Lion advised, 'those who are opposed the name, please raise your hands.' Again, the rhino counted the hands from one side, the cheetah on the other, and the eagle from the sky.

The lion asked the rhino to declare the result of the election. While the voting and counting was going on, the lion noticed a number of hungry carnivorous animals were looking at some of the herbivorous animals with dubious eyes and were sitting questionably close to them. Mr Lion could read their intention and gave an angry look before saying, 'Will you please behave yourselves! You are going to create suspicion and distrust!'

Mr Rhino declared that those in support of the name totalled 78,429 whilst those against totalled 7,653. The name was then accepted by a majority of 70,776 votes.

Some of the animals objected, suggesting that the election was not a democratic one. A number of animals were absent and their vote was considered important. Others stated that the counting had not been accurate.

The rhino's temper rose to his face, but he suppressed his emotion and fought back his words. He did not like his authority being challenged, and so said loudly to the lion, 'I will challenge anybody with the count. The majority was over seventy-thousand. How can anybody suggest the counting was not accurate? If the majority was marginal, recounting could be done, but there is no question of recounting or as to the re-selection of a name. Moreover, those who are absent have been informed of our desire to have them attend the meeting and they have chosen not to attend.'

Mr Lion nodded patiently.

The rhino continued, 'Mr President, ask somebody who is good at counting and I won't be able to be on the committee in the future.'

Mr Lion responded, 'Calm down. Don't take this as a personal attack. The majority of the animals and I have full trust in you.' He then turned his attention towards the animals. 'We must respect the majority verdict. The name of the association has been decided by the majority of seventy- thousand seven hundred and seventy-six votes. We are now referred to as the Masa Mara Animals Association.'

There was a huge, deafening applaud of paws and hooves.

The lion thanked everybody and said, 'Our next agenda for discussion is to form a committee.'

An ostrich looked puzzled, almost as if he had lost his way and suddenly been thrown into the middle of the meeting. He was hearing lots of new words that he never heard before. Inside, he was feeling foolish, but made the decision to satisfy his curiosity. Suddenly he asked, 'But what is a committee? I think I have come to the wrong place—perhaps I am uninvited. I am sorry to say that politics is not in my blood!'

There was a harsh bark of laughter from various groups of animal.

Mr Lion had learnt, over the past two days, when to talk softly and when to roar. He said politely, 'My friends, you shouldn't laugh at anyone!' He then directed his attention back to the ostrich and replied, 'You are in right place. I have invited all the creatures living in Maasai Mark Park to attend this meeting.' He then added, 'a committee is a group of people in our committee, a group of animals or creatures selected to do a particular job. Some members will be chosen to negotiate with the Maasai Mara Park Authority, for example.' He then turned to the masses. 'I feel that a small committee is good for making swift decisions and taking quick action. I propose a committee of five members who are sincere, honest, hard-working and would work voluntarily. You might have to compromise your family life for the organisation. Family members will also need to adjust and sacrifice the sake of the organisation.

'The posts I propose are as follows: firstly, the role of the president or chairperson. Secondly, a secretary. Third, an accountant. And fourth, two other ordinary members. I leave it open for you to select or elect five members.'

Discussion quickly began with an excited tone echoing around the animals. A leopard said, 'I feel a committee of only five members won't be adequate for our organisation of over a thousand. A president or chairperson needs an assistant. I propose that we also have a president/chairperson assistant, as well as a secretary assistant.' He received good support and his proposal was accepted.

The wildebeest said, 'I feel like an accountant would also need an assistant to keep a record of all the members. It is not an easy job, and so he or she would definitely need an assistant!' This suggestion was also accepted.

The zebra said, 'Mr Chairperson, I am sincere and hard-working, and I would like to put myself forward for the role of Assistant General Secretary.'

'Oh?' said a giraffe, giving the zebra a dirty look. 'You consider yourself to be hard-working?'

Another long-necked spotted giraffe, standing at a height of approximately 12 feet tall, said, 'I also work very hard for my living, Mr Chairperson. I am sincere, honest and good looking.' Everybody, including Mr Lion, laughed.

Somebody commented, 'If you are good looking, we all are also good looking!'

When the laughter finally stopped, he turned to Mr Lion and said, 'Mr President, have I said something wrong?'

'No, not at all,' he responded. 'We are not here to criticise others. Everybody has the equal right to express their views. We must try to appreciate others. We all have lots of good qualities and, at the same time, some bad qualities. My friends, so as not to find faults in others, try to spot faults in yourselves and correct them so that you are a good person.'

In the recent days, Mr Lion had learnt to be careful with his tone, and that there was a time and a place for a roar.

The giraffe then said, 'Can I make a request? I want to be your assistant, Mr Chairperson.'

The hippopotamus said, 'I feel we need proportional representation—at least one member from each community.'

The crocodile said, 'It would not be possible to have representation from each and every community of animals and birds. The committee would grow be too big, and it would be difficult to run the meetings. You would need to decide how many members you want from larger animals, how many from birds and how many from amphibious reptiles like us, and then how many from herbivorous animals.'

Discussion then ensued, but no decision was made. Time was running out, and the safari cars would soon invade the park once again.

The lion adjourned the meeting for the day and summarised the decision that had been made before saying, 'Thank you friends! Today's meeting is over as it is now time for the safari cars to come back into our homeland. You chose the name of our organisation to be the Maasai Mara Animals Association. We will meet here again tomorrow at the same time to form a committee. Now, go home safely and think about whom should be part of the committee and who can lead the association forward.'

The meeting was closed, and so the lion said, 'You have two hours to reach home before any animal can attack you. He asked the unwell leopard to wait and advised that somebody would help him to return home and arrange food for him. 'You can stay with me in my den,' Mr Lion offered, wanting to extend his friendship to the leopard.

The leopard replied, 'You are very a kind and tender-hearted creation. Still, I am managing myself. The only problem I have is that I cannot hunt and so I remain hungry most of the days.'

Mr Lion said, 'Do not worry. I will send food for you.'

Mr Leopard said to Mr Lion, 'My son and daughter-in-law may not like it. They will think I am begging for food from you. It will hurt their pride. I know as a friend and neighbour you want to help others, but people might think differently.'

All of the lion's supporters were impressed upon hearing their leader offering to send food to the older leopard until the food supplies would come from the Safari Park Authority.

Like the previous day, Mr Lion discussed with his supporters the next day's meeting. He returned to his den as quickly as he could. His partner noticed he was in a delighted mood; relaxed and calm. She knew the meeting had been successful. His wives asked him how the meeting had gone. He informed them that he was happy with its progress and then went on to discuss his plans for the future. He said to them, 'I was very hurt hearing the poorly leopard's cry. He came to me and told me his family had abandoned him because he's infirm. He told me he'd die of hunger. Tears flowed from many animals' eyes. And so I have decided to send him food until we get supplies from the 'Safari Park Authority. I therefore request that you deliver some food to the leopard,' he told one of his wives.

His two grandsons said they, too, wanted to go. Mr Lion agreed that they could go.

One of his grandsons said, 'I will teach his son and daughter-in-law a lesson.'

Mr Lion said, 'Please do not dare say anything or do anything silly to him.'

One of his wives said, 'No, they will not say or do anything silly. I will see to that.'

On the way to the leopard's den, the lioness was apprehensive and on the lookout for the leopards being hostile towards her and the cubs. Upon reaching the leopard's den, the lioness called, 'Mr Leopard, we have come at the request of Mr Lion, your president. He has sent some food for you. Please accept it.'

Mr Leopard appeared and said, 'Please do come in.'

The lioness nodded before stating, 'We are in hurry. We will come in future. Now we are friends so we will meet you again soon.'

She left the place quickly, before any incident could unfold if the leopard's family was to become hostile.

Returning from the leopard's den, the lioness explained to her husband what she had seen at the leopard's home. She had heard some yelling and raised voices, and she had understood that she and the cubs were not welcome by the leopard's son and daughter-in-law; they had refused to accept the food, growling and hissing that they are capable of looking after their father. They stated that he had gone 'insane' and was suffering from 'brain degeneration'. Mr leopard had refuted this, stating that he was far from insane but rather just hungry.

'Give me the food my friend Mr Lion has sent for me!' he had demanded. 'Don't take it away!'

'I left the food there and came back,' said the lioness.

Mr Lion said, 'I don't know what else we can do for the helpless leopard.'

One of his grandsons interjected, 'The leopard is naughty! He is not looking after his dad! I wanted to swipe him!'

Mr Lion said, 'I am sure you will not do that to me or to your parents!'

'Certainly not!' was the response.

Mr Lion slept well that night and awoke early in the morning, fresh and prepared for the day's meeting. His thoughts were interrupted by his grandchildren's pestering for him to play with them, but he did not mind. He played and tumbled with them for a while, delighting in their happiness.

Chapter 3:
Committee Formation

The meeting started at the defined place and time. 'Dear friends,' Mr Lion began, 'I welcome you to today's meeting. I am very pleased to see you all here today in such a large number. Please, take your seat and be comfortable.

'The purpose underpinning today's meeting is the need to form a committee' Yesterday you chose the name of our organisation. We are now a big family, and in a family everybody is equal. Nobody should feel that their interest has been neglected or compromised or that we are not represented in the committee. Whatever the size and shape of the committee, the prime interest should be to look after the interests of the Maasai Mara animals, birds, reptiles and other residents of the park, including the Maasai people.

'I want a bond with every creature in the park. I want us to be able to run this organisation smoothly. It is a job with huge responsibility. And, as discussed yesterday, we all might have to sacrifice our personal and family interests for the sake of the organisation. I would request that you select twenty members for the committee. We will need a president/chairperson, a vice-president/vice chairperson, a secretary, an assistant secretary, an accountant, and an assistant accountant. That's a total of six posts, whilst the remaining fourteen posts will be ordinary members. I leave it open to the general members to choose the candidates. There will then be a vote by the raising of hands. First, we need to select a president.'

The lion's name was proposed by an elephant.

'What are the duties of the president, secretary and others?' a cheetah asked.

'Very good question,' the lion replied. 'That leads me to a very important point that, once the committee is formed, we will need to create the constitution and outline the duties of all the members. This will be written in the constitution.'

Some birds then asked, 'What is the const—?'

'The constitution details the written rules and regulations. For example, it might outline the duty of a president and the duty of the secretary, and maybe the role to be adopted by other committee members, etcetera.'

The Rhino said, 'I think we need to have the consti...—Whatever it is!—first, and then we can select who we consider to be a fit candidate for the post.'

A number of the other animals also suggested writing the constitution before forming the executive committee.

'Do you know, friends, to write the constitution is not an easy job and it cannot be done in a hurry,' said Mr Lion. 'When we form the committee, the committee will write the constitution, taking into account the aims and objectives, possible legal matters and proper wording.' A great deal of argument and discussion ensued, with Mr Lion eventually interrupting, stating, 'Well, I will describe in short the roles of President, Secretary and other members.

'First and foremost, the role of the president is the head of the organisation—almost like the head of the family. He conducts the committee meetings. He asks the general secretary to call the meetings whenever this is considered necessary. He negotiates with other organisations. He has the power to make decisions in discussions with the secretary and the other committee members. In the case of the secretary role, this individual calls the meetings and partakes in discussions with the president. He keeps a record of the meetings and accordingly prepares the agenda of the meeting with discussions with the president, and accordingly informs the general public about the decision taken by the committee. He communicates with the other organisations. Moreover, he also keeps up-to-date records of the members. Third, in the case of the role of the accountant, we have over one-hundred-thousand members, and the membership is constantly changing. The accountant's job is to keep records of the members and inform the general secretary and president accordingly. The members' role is to help the president and secretary to make any difficult decisions.

'Each of these posts is very important, particularly in the case of the president, secretary and accountant. When the committee is formed, the committee will write the constitution.

'Now, we must decide who will be your president, secretary and other members. Before then, however, would you like to call your leader president or chairperson?'

'Well, friends, we don't sit on a chair, we sit on hay, so the title should be Hayperson and not Chairperson!' said a nameless animal.

Mr President and many other animals chuckled.

'And what is more, we are not a person, and so I would say it more appropriate to use president,' suggested Mr Duma.

Mrs Kiboko said, 'No, I feel chairperson is a beautiful name and we should use that.'

Discussions and arguments continued, with various group of animal suggesting various things.

Mr Tembo raised his head. 'I feel the name should be appropriate for our organisation and should be appealing to the Safari Park Authority. The word 'president' has got a certain gravity to it. I will request all the residents of the park call our leader President.'

After a long and heated debate, it was agreed by Mr Lion that 'This proposal can now be accepted!'

Many animals shouted, 'Mr Lion, you are our president! You are our president!'

The lion responded, 'This is not the way to elect your representatives. The procedure requires that one of you propose the name of a candidate and another person supports him. The candidate should accept such a proposal. If there is no other candidate, he or she will then be elected for the post. If there is more than one candidate for the same post, voting will then take place by the raising of hands.'

The elephant proposed the lion Mr Simba be chosen for the post of President, with the giraffe supporting this. The leopard proposed the cheetah Mr Duma with the hyena supporting this. There was no other name proposed. Voting took place with the raising of hands. The lion, Mr Simba, achieved 40,284 votes whilst the cheetah, Mr Duma, received 2,083 votes. There were a lot of animals absent. The total number of votes cast totalled 42,367.

'Mr Simba is elected through a majority of 38,246 votes!'

The various members congratulated Mr Simba. There was a loud applause for him.

Mr Simba thanked every animal with a big smile on his face, thankful for being elected as their president. His roaring voice echoed deep into the field and forests, and then he said, 'Mark my words: I will try my best to have our food supplied by the Park Authority.' He received another loud applause and three cheers.

Mr Duma congratulated Mr Simba on his success and assured everybody that he would work for the animal organisation to the benefit of society.

When it came to election for the post of Vice President, the leopard, Mr Chui, was proposed by Hyena, with Mr Mbwa seconding the proposal. There was no other candidate, and so the leopard was chosen as Vice President.

Election for the post of General Secretary involved the elephant, Mr Tembo, as proposed by the gazelle, with the zebra seconding this. The hyena mentioned the name the buffalo, Mr Nyati, with the cheetah, Duma, supporting this. Voting took place. Mr Tembo received the most votes from the herbivorous animal and birds, equating to a total of 42,679, whilst Mr Nyati, the buffalo, received 3,287, making a majority of 39,392. The total number of votes cast equalled 45,966, with Mr Tembo elected as General Secretary.

For the post of Assistant General Secretary, the giraffe, Mr Twiga, was put forward by a bird known as Kori Bustard, which was seconded by a guinea-fowl. The zebra, Mr Pundamilia, was proposed by the gazelle, which was seconded by a bird known as Lilac.

Voting took place and Mr Twiga received 41,322 votes whilst Mr Pundamilia, the zebra, received 6,302. Mr Twiga was elected by a majority of 35,020, with the total number of votes cast amounting to 47,624.

For the post of Accountant, the rhino was proposed by a lion and seconded by an elephant. No other candidate was suggested, and so the rhino was elected to the role.

For the post of Assistant Accountant, the eagle's name was proposed by the buffalo and seconded by the jackal. No other names were put forward, and so the eagle was elected without any opposition.

The lion then stated, 'There are 14 posts of ordinary committee members. Should more than 14 names be proposed, we will need a vote, otherwise all the proposed candidates will be elected unopposed. Please put your name forward if you would be interested in adopting the role.'

A number of names were put forward for voting, including Impala (Swala-Pala), a dog known as Mbwa, Cheetah (Mr Duma), Gazelle (Miss Swala), Wildebeest (Mr Nyumbu), a bird known as the Weaver Bird, the hippopotamus (Mr Kiboko), crocodile (Mrs Mamba), zebra (Mr Pundamilia), Lilac-breasted Roller (Miss Coracias), deer (Miss Pala Hala), buffalo (Mr Nyati), eagle (Miss Tia), hyena (Mrs Fisi) and rhinoceros (Mr Kifaru).

A total of fourteen names were proposed for the fourteen posts, meaning all candidates were elected as committee members. A few posts were reserved for co-opted members.

The President, Mr Simba, then said, 'In the future, if the committee feels like we should take on more members, this will benefit the organisation. The committee can then approve the candidates as co-opted members.' He then went on to state, 'We have to take the Maasai People in our committee.' The president then congratulated all the successful candidates elected to the committee and thanked everybody for their time. He said victoriously, 'With your help, support and cooperation, we will pressurise the Safari Park Authority to supply our food from the authority.' Mr president then summarised the decision of the general public. He read the names of all of the committee members elected and asked them to stand beside him so that everybody was able to see their faces and remember them. He then declared the meeting closed.

Mr President informed the newly elected committee members that there would be a committee meeting on Saturday October 23, 2010, at 10am, located beside the River Mara in an area of dense bush where no safari car could invade to disrupt the meeting. 'As you know,' he advised, 'you have two hours to reach your home and no animal will attack you before this time has expired.'

All the committee members, particularly Mr Simba and Mr Tembo, relaxed for one full week as a result of all of the intense and difficult discussion with various classes of animals the previous few days. Mr Simba was tired; he needed a good few days' rest to recharge his batteries.

Later that evening, he laid outside his den on thick grassland in his comfortable bed beside the River Mara watching the sunset. He remembered the first time he had watched such a beautiful sunset and spent an evening with his eldest wife many years before. Then, all of a sudden, the series of events that had unfolded the past few days appeared again in his mind's eye. He felt deeply for the infirm leopard. And then he remembered his first wife's death, which happened as she hunted with him; he had been unable to save her. She was deeply injured and did not recover from her injuries, as inflicted by a wildebeest. The wildebeest was also killed in the same attack.

But she had not died of hunger. Still, he visited the place where his first spouse had died many years ago. Thinking of all of the incidents that had happened in the past, he went into a deep sleep.

~*~*~*~

Mr Lion woke the next morning, fresh and welcoming the dawn. He went for a walk, made plans for the next committee meeting, and thought deeply about what to write in the constitution. He was so deeply involved in his thoughts that he forgot to go hunting with his wives. His wives were very understanding—they knew their husband was now holding a very responsible position in the Animal Society and needed their support. Since Mr Simba had become the president of the organisation, he had not had the time to look after his wives. Nonetheless, they felt proud as wives of the president.

During the next few days, Mr Lion was so much absorbed in his work that, at various times, he forgot to go for dinner. His youngest wife was very caring and brought food to him where he was working. His love for his younger wife increased enormously. This is not to say, however, that his love for his other wives diminished; he knew very well that if he was to neglect his other wives, they would then go to some other handsome, young, caring and strong lion who could protect them. Mr Lion couldn't and wouldn't allow that to happen. It would decrease his image. And now that every animal recognised him as their president, he had a reputation to uphold, which he could never and would never allow to be discredited.

Chapter 4:
The First Committee Meeting

On Saturday October 23, 2010, the first committee meeting was held at the scheduled time and in the venue decided upon during the previous meeting. The herbivorous animals were scared, with the zebra saying to the impala, 'Do you think we will be alive after this meeting? Could this be a trap for us?'

The impala replied confirming that he, too, was worried. 'We will go to the meeting with Mr Elephant,' he suggested. 'He will definitely protect us in case we are attacked by any carnivorous animal during the meeting.' Many herbivorous animals sat close to Mr Elephant, keeping their distance from the carnivorous animals.

The President, Mr Simba, welcomed all of the members to the first committee meeting and asked them to take their respected seats and get comfortable. 'I am glad to see you all present in our first committee meeting,' he said. 'You must be thrilled. This is your first meeting with different classes of animal, all of whom your enemy yesterday. They are now sitting beside you and talking to you. This is a monumental event. We are going to change society! The whole system needs change! And very soon, we will all play together, eat together, sing together, and have fun together!

'You all are holding a responsible position in the committee.' He then went on to say, 'Very soon you will learn how the committee runs, how to behave in and outside of the committee. You are holding a respectable position in our community. You are a role model for others—others who would like to follow your ideal! The future of our organisation depends on your decisions and actions! The discussion we are having here is private and confidential, and it should not be disclosed to your wife or husband, to your friends, relatives, or even to the general public unless we decide to do so.

'Our first task is to write the rules and regulations, which all the animals of Maasai Mara will follow. This is called the Constitution. This comprises the aims and objectives of the association, the duties of the committee members, and the rules and regulations of the organisation.

'I have explained to you in short the duties of the president and secretary. Today we will discuss the other issues; this will be legally binding.' Mr Simba then explained what he thought about the constitution. The elephant, Mr Tembo, and the other committee members wrote up the Constitution, which was then read, with everybody accepting everything that had been detailed: .

1. Organisation's name:

The Maasai Mara Animals Association.

2. The objectives of the organisation:
   a. To improve the health and wellbeing of all the creatures living in this park, including the Maasai People.
   b. To improve the relationship of all the animals, birds, reptiles and other creatures living both within the park and outside of the park.
   c. To have medical facilities and vaccination programmes for all the residents of this park and the Maasai People.

d. To improve the living environment in the park and the Maasai Villages.
e. To have in place recreation and entertainment facilities for all.
f. To implement the rule that no animal will kill any other animal or human to enable them to live or for fun, either in the park or outside of the park.
g. To ensure a non-violent way of living.
h. To help others in need.

3. Membership:

The membership of the organisation shall be open to all creatures living in and around the park. They must enrol their name in the organisation.

4. Termination of membership:

Membership will be terminated if a member's activities are contrary to the objectives of the association or if his or her activities bring the name of the association into disrepute. If his or her activities are detrimental to the organisation, he or she will then not be permitted to live in the park.

5. Committee's function:

5.1 The executive committee will look after the best interests of the Association.

5.2 Negotiations with The Maasai Mara Park Authority will be ongoing, focused on the wellbeing of all residents in the park.

5.3 The Committee will have regular meetings.

5.4 The Committee will have the power to punish any member breaching the peace or not obeying the constitution or displaying violent behaviour.

5.5 Members are required to attend committee meetings.

6. Duties of the officers:

    a. President and Vice President

6.1 The President is the head of the organisation and will preside at all meetings.

6.2 The Vice President will look after the president's office in his absence.

    b. The General Secretary and Assistant General Secretary

6.3 Will call all meetings, giving appropriate notice.

6.4 Will maintain a register of the association and the minutes of the meetings.

6.5 The Assistant General Secretary will look after the Office of Secretary in his absence.

c. The Accountant and Assistant Accountant

6.6 Will maintain a register of all the members of the association.

6.7 Will produce the list of members in the annual general meeting.

d. Executive members

6.8 Will assist the President and committee at times of need.

6.9 Any member failing to attend the committee meetings without prior notification warrant the committee to expel him from the committee and co-opt another member in his place.

This constitution was adopted on October 23, 2010 by the following:

1] Mr L. Simba: President of Maasai Mara Animals Association.

2] Mr E. Tembo: General Secretary of Maasai Mara Animal Association.

President Mr Simba, declared the meeting closed and informed the group that their next meeting would be held on Wednesday November

3, 2010, at 10am, notably in the same location, with the objective to write a letter to the Maasai Mara Safari Park Authority.

Chapter 5:
The Second Committee Meeting

The meeting could not start in time due to some members being absent. Secretary Mr Tembo informed the committee that no committee member had apologised to him for, or explained, their absence. President Mr Simba advised the committee members of the duty of the committee members to inform the Secretary or President if any member would be unable to attend the committee meeting. He also advised the members that a minimum of fifty percent of the total number of committee members need be present to constitute a valid meeting.

'This is known as a quorum,' he stated. 'For today's meeting, a minimum of ten members need to be present; however, we have only eight members at present. The meeting cannot start unless two more members arrive to form the quorum. We will wait for a few more minutes.'

A few members attended late and apologised to the President. Miss Swala entered huffing and puffing, soaked and frightened, and breathless. All the committee members were astonished and puzzled.

Mr Simba asked her, 'What happened?'

She took a good few minutes to get her breath back and replied slowly, 'The reason for my being late is that I am lucky to be alive! I was attacked by a wild cat on the way here! I ran for my life. He even chased me up to the edge of the River Mara! I had no other alternative but to jump into the river! I was carried away by the water current away from the mouth of the hungry wild cat! I knew very well that I would be eaten by Crocodile should I need to do that! I was lucky that all the crocodiles were, at that time, taking nap on the other bank of the river! I swam quickly before a crocodile could see me in the water. Finally, the cat gave up chasing me as he could not catch me!

'Mr President,' she continued, 'you must stop this type of incident from happening in the future!'

The President was very angry, which was apparent on his face. He said the criminal would need to be punished.

She continued, also stating that it would be very difficult for us to attend any meeting in the future if she was to be harassed or attacked on the way to committee meetings.

'This venue for committee meetings is not a very safe place for us,' she told him. 'We have to pass through lots of carnivorous animals' dens! Track number 96 is a notorious track, with many innocent animals known to have lost their lives in this track! You may be aware that this track extends from one end of the park to the other, from north to south, and is very near to the River Mara where it takes a sharp ninety-degree right-turn. Either side of this track is covered with tall and thick straw-coloured dry grasses, matching the colour of the big cats. It is an ideal place for them to camouflage themselves and ambush their pray! What's more, the river is full of crocodiles! If your foot slips and you lose your balance and fall into the river, there is no chance you will come out of the water alive!

'With this said, I request you change the venue!'

A number of the other committee members agreed with her proposal.

The Second Committee Meeting

Committee member Mr Nyumbu said, 'Mr President, I feel this has been an intentional attack on Miss Swala On Election Day, Mr Duma and a few other carnivorous animals opposed your proposal, and they were unhappy as they couldn't secure a position on our committee. They were defeated by other members. I have heard they are trying to form an opposition group.'

The meeting started half an hour late. Mr Simba apologised to Miss Swala for the incident and promised to issue badges for the members to attend the committee meetings so that no animal could attack any committee member when on the way to attend. Alternatively, they would look for a suitable, safer place for the committee meetings to be held.

Mr Simba started the meeting by expressing his sadness. He also felt bad for the poor wildcat who had attacked the committee member Miss Swala. He said, 'The poor cat must be very hungry, which is why he's attacked Miss Swala. We should meet him after the meeting and enquire as to the reason behind this; if necessary, we must then provide him with food.

'Dear friends,' he continued, 'today's meeting is concerned with drafting a letter to the Maasai Mara Safari Park Authority.'

The first problem to arise was that nobody knew the address of where the letter should be sent. Mr Simba asked, 'Does anybody know the safari park's office address?

'You know, I am the tallest animal in the park,' Mr Twiga said. 'I can see the horizon when I raise my head. I have seen where the safari park office is situated, although I do not know the address.

All committee members laughed.

Mr President said, 'Do not insult or laugh when somebody speaks in the committee meeting.'

Mr Tembo responded with, 'We all know where it is situated, but we need the address to send a letter.'

'I have got something to suggest to you, Mr President,' Miss Swala said to the committee.

'What is your proposal, Miss Swala?' asked Mr Simba.

She said, 'I feel the letter can be delivered personally by hand to the office.'

'Without an address?' Mr Tembo asked, coolly.

'No, we could go there to deliver the letter and then ask the address and write the address before delivering the letter,' she confirmed.

Mr Simba accepted the proposal, and said, 'Why not?' as there was no other alternative.

Mr Simba's worst fear centred on the issue of how to communicate with the park authority. A strange and unpleasant fear developed in his mind, one which he could not explain to himself. The problem was who would write the letter and in what language? English, local Maasai (Maa) or animal language? And if the latter, which animal? Lion, elephant, cheetah, rhino or birds? The authority would not be able to read or understand any animal language or the content of the letter, and so the letter would just land in the bin!

Mr Simba asked the committee members for any suggestions. Disappointment lay like a thick cloud over the committee. There was a lot of discussion, argument and suggestion, all presented by various members. A member of the committee made a stupid suggestion and insisted that his idea was brilliant and stated that the committee should accept it. Mr Simba raised his eyebrow and said,

'Thank you for your thoughtful suggestion, but I don't think this is a good suggestion for acceptance by the committee.'

The majority nodded their heads. Almost every member put forward their views, but none were acceptable to the president or the other members.

Mr Simba suggested that 'There is a need for us to understand the Maasai people's body language and they ours, so why should we not approach the Maasai leader who knows English or otherwise use his local language Maa?'

Everybody was greatly pleased and excited, which was a huge relief to the president. That was the best suggestion, and almost everybody accepted the proposal by nodding their head. Mr Simba asked other committee members if they had considered any other alternatives and then suggested they put them forward to the committee for discussion.

He looked around at all the committee members. 'Are there any other alternatives?'

The cheetah then asked, 'Who will approach the Maasai leader? I am willing to go but, being carnivorous, they might be frightened and our plan might fail. I feel no carnivorous animal should approach them. They might kill us and our mission would be a failure.'

Mr Nyumbu volunteered to go to the Maasai village on the behalf of the 'committee.

'It is very kind of you to offer your services for the organisation,' Mr Simba began, 'but I personally do not feel you should go. He also said, 'It would not be a good idea to send any ferocious carnivorous animal.'

Tia asked, 'Why can't she go?'

The Maasai people might get frightened, causing our objective to fail, which nobody would want,' advised Mr President.

It was decided that only non-aggressive carnivorous or herbivorous animals and birds would approach the humans. The committee decided that the General Secretary, Mr Tembo, Miss Swala and a beautiful bird named the coracias would approach the Maasai leader and invite him to attend the next committee meeting with the aim of discussing the matter. The meeting would take place on Saturday November 20, 2010, notably at the same venue.

'If we can manage to acquire friendship with them, our objective could be achieved. If they decline to help us, we need to think about how we could communicate with the authority,' the president advised.

A number of committee members suggested that, before heading to the Maasai Village, they should inform the Maasai people that a delegate would be arriving for friendship.

'As we are their enemy,' one said, 'they might kill us if we go there uninvited and without previous notice.'

Mr Simba agreed on this point, and so it was decided that the eagle would send the message from Mr President to the Maasai people using the sky.

Mr Lion closed the meeting and said, 'Our next meeting will be held on November 20, 2010.'

Mr Simba and few other members spent one full day sitting beside the river, planning the friendship meeting with the Maasai people. They discussed how they would approach the leader and what they would propose, and how they would convince them.'

The Second Committee Meeting

'You know, we will just have to try to persuade the Maasai people that they will benefit joining us,' said Mr Simba to Mr Tembo.

CHAPTER 6:
A FRIENDSHIP WITH
THE MAASAI COMMUNITY

Two days later, on a beautiful Friday morning as the sun was rising in the east, turning the sky red, as planned, Secretary Mr Tembo, Miss Swala and a charming bird known as Miss Coracias slowly approached the Maasai village. Some of the Maasai people were grazing their herds in a pasture just outside the park. From a distance, the Maasai people saw two animals and a bird fly towards them in a jolly mood.

The coracias was riding on the back of the elephant and Miss Swala was walking beside them. The charming bird flew and sat on the right shoulder of one of the Maasai people and sang a song in her melodious voice. She behaved in a friendly manner and informed the man that she was his friend. From a distance, the gazelle danced, the elephant raised his trunk and said, 'Hello!' in his friendly trumpeting sound — the sound with which the Maasais are all acquainted. The Maasai people knew and understood the body language of the elephants and other animals, whether the animal was friend or foe.

The Maasai people knew a delegate was coming from the animals society to discuss the possibility of a friendship. They were expecting a ferocious animal, like a lion, leopard or cheetah, but they were surprised to see birds, elephants and antelope coming for friendship. They were mesmerised as to why, all of a sudden, the three animals were there.

'What could they want?' they wondered.

The elephant pointed his trunk to the approaching Safari jeep and made a noise like a warning. The Maasai people turned their heads and saw many safari jeeps approaching the park. The elephant kicked dust from the ground and threw more in the air before beginning to cough. The bird also stopped singing and started coughing, pretending to choke.

The elephant showed the Maasai people using his body language that they should stop the safari jeeps from visiting the park. In time, they managed to convey their message, emphasising that the safari jeeps were not welcome in the park.

The Maasai people asked them if anything was wrong in the park. Miss Swala said, 'Yes,' nodding her head.

They then managed to convey a message to the Maasai people that they were invited to attend a meeting on November 20, 2010 at the safari park.

'We need your help,' they told them with their body language.

A few curious Maasai people came to find out what the animals were talking about. The elephant showed that they were having difficulty breathing because of the pollution created by the car engines. The bird further told them, 'I cannot sing in a melodious voice! The pollution from the cars chokes me and causing me to lose my melodious voice! I am sure you are having similar problems. They have polluted our rivers, particularly the River Mara.'

The Maasai people understood the problem of the animals and agreed that they were also having similar problems.

The elephant said, 'Together, we can stop them from coming here. We need your help and you need ours. We used to live in peace and harmony with a tranquil land, and we did so for many centuries. We consider you to be our friends. So please join with us. We are having a meeting on Saturday November 20, 2010 on the bank of the River Mara.

'You are stretching your hands to us for help... Why suddenly this change of heart? You don't allow us to graze our herd in your park, so why then would we help you?' one of the Maasai asked in surprise.

Mr Tembo introduced Miss Pala, Miss Coracias and himself to the other Maasai people and said politely, 'All the creatures living in the park have united and come together to form a committee. We want you to join us so that we can all live in peace.

'The world is changing. We were neighbours before but now we are friends. You can bring your herd into the park and no animal will attack you. This is our promise to you.

'May I request that you attend a meeting on November 20, 2010 at our place? Mr Simba, our president, will explain all about our peaceful mission. We three will also come to you on the day to escort you to our committee meeting, where we will discuss all the problems we are facing and try to arrive at an amicable solution.

'We would be delighted if you attend the meeting.'

Other Maasai men and women watched from a distance as a few of their friends communicated with the animals and birds. They could not stay away and wanted to know what was going on and so ran towards their friends.

'Many thanks for listening to us.' said Mr Tembo.

'Goodbye! See you on Saturday!' said all three animals.

Mr Tembo's immediate impression was that the Maasai people had agreed to the proposal. He addressed his friends Miss Swala and Miss Coracias, stating, 'I am pleased! I think we have managed to convey our messages!'

Miss Swala said, 'I feel they're not happy with the safari jeeps coming to their land either.'

Miss Coracias asked, 'Do you think they will attend our meeting?'

'I feel the Maasai people have accepted our invitation and will attend the committee meeting,' said Mr Tembo.

Returning from the Maasai village, all three went straight to Mr Simba to inform him about their successful mission. Mr Simba was eagerly waiting for the good news. He said, 'Welcome, everybody! Please be seated and comfortable!'

Mr Tembo explained the discussion they had had with the Maasai people, telling Mr Simba all about everything that was said. 'I am confident they will attend our meeting, and at that point we will have to convince them how they are going to benefit from our friendship.'

Some discussion followed but this could not continue long as Mr Tembo saw that a number of the safari jeeps were approaching them. He informed Mr Simba, who said, 'You must be tired as you travelled early dawn to the Maasai village, so please go home and take some rest. Tomorrow we will discuss and make plans as to how we will present our case to the Maasai people. Thank you so much for your hard work!'

Chapter 7:
The Committee Meeting with the Maasai Leader

It was a pleasant Saturday when the meeting took place on November 20, 2010 at the scheduled time and place. The previous night, there was heavy rainfall and, as a result, water had collected on the safari jeeps' track in a number of different places. Animal delegates, namely Mr Tembo and his friends, went to escort the Maasai villagers to the venue where the meeting was to be held, and it was there that they saw a thirsty lioness drinking water from the track.

Mr Tembo said to his companion, 'It seems she has just finished her breakfast and is having her tea.' Everybody laughed but silently so as not to alert the lioness or disturb her drinking.

The lioness saw the animals and the Maasai people passing through. She lifted her head, nodded to them, and then smiled at them. Mr Tembo and the others also nodded at her. Seeing this, the Maasai people's immediate impression of the ferocious animals was that their behaviour had changed. They were amazed to see the animals' friendship with one another.

The lioness did not show any indication of hostility to the strangers passing so close to her. Delicious food, human, easy pray within her grasp. In fact, she was not concerned at all. This behaviour impressed the Maasai people.

Early morning, a very thirsty lioness drinking water from a safari jeep's tracks

'Why are you drinking dirty water from here? Mr Tembo asked the lioness. 'Surely you will fall ill. Please go and drink fresh and clean water from the river.'

'Thank you, friends, for your kind advice,' she responded, 'but to go to River Mara I have to travel through many other carnivorous animals' territory. This would be treated as trespassing and I could be prosecuted for that.'

Mr Tembo, Miss Swala and Miss Coracias escorted the delegate from the Maasai village to the venue. It was a long road from the Maasai village to the venue.

Mr Simba and other committee members were eagerly awaiting their arrival. Finally, Mr Tembo introduced the Maasai delegates to the committee.

'Mr O'Dingo Maasai leader, Mr Amolo and Mr O'Ginga, this is our president, Mr Simba, and our committee members.'

Mr Simba asked everybody to sit and make themselves comfortable. He asked the committee members to introduce themselves, which they did.

Mr Simba then opened the meeting. 'Dear friends,' he began, 'I welcome you to our committee meeting. We are privileged to have with us such honourable members from the Maasai community, who have been good enough to attend our meeting. We have been neighbours over many centuries, but in the past we have never communicated with one another, nor have we tried to understand each other. We instead chose to create a hostile atmosphere and looked at each other as an enemy. We fought amongst ourselves for various reasons. We kept ourselves isolated and separated, and remained divided.

'Now, however, this world is progressing very quickly and is getting smaller and smaller. You may have seen and heard that neighbouring countries have joined to form a federation and are helping each other to live in harmony and peace, learning each other's cultures and language so as to facilitate better communication. The whole world is a big family. There is no need for war, for violence.

'What is more, we have a plan to stop killing any animal or human for the sake of living. Now is the time to live together in harmony and peace, to cooperate with one another in need.' He also went on to say, 'We don't live for ourselves but for others.

'Now, dear Maasai friends, we have formed a committee to protest the safari jeeps entering our homeland and disturbing the peace and tranquility, polluting the air and endangering our lives. We also want our food supply to come from the Safari Park Authority. If they want visitors to come here and enjoy watching our way of living, then we have a demand, and it is our fundamental right to demand this from the park authority. We want improvements to our and your own health.'

The president's speech was translated by the secretary, Mr Tembo and the other animals using body language, which was communicated to the Maasai delegates. It was anybody's guess how much they understood! But nonetheless, it was quite impressive to the Maasai people.

Mr President said, 'We feel you are also having a similar problem. We want to protest about this and we need your help to do that to the best possible extent. I will sincerely request of the Maasai leader, Mr O'Dingo, that we know your views in this matter.'

The Maasai leader said, 'Mr President, dear friends, thank you for inviting us to your committee meeting. It is our pleasure to attend. What I have understood from your conversation is that you have decided to stop the safari jeeps from entering the park and you'd like to take action against the Safari Park Authority... You want improvements to be made to the park and for the wellbeing of the animals and the Maasai people.

'Well, I am pleased to see your enthusiasm, unity and nonviolence approach. We are willing to help you in this good cause of yours, but there is a problem, and that is the language barrier.'

Mr President nodded thoughtfully and said, 'Of course, I agree. It is an obstacle. Gradually, however, it is our hope that we can overcome this. We will need to learn each other's language. Moreover, you will benefit from our friendship and cooperation.'

The Maasai leader asked, 'But, Mr President, would you explain to me how?'

He smiled in response. 'The Safari Park Authority must have earned millions of shillings from the travellers each and every year for the last who-knows-how-many years. What they have spent for your or our benefit is negligible. They failed to invest any money in improving your health or indeed our own. We have discussed this in our committee meeting and we feel we should demand improvement to everyone's health, provided by the Safari Park Authority. It is our fundamental right, and we are to demand this of the Park Authority.

'However, we cannot succeed alone, so, if you agree, together we can then form a united force to negotiate with the authority. Moreover, you live just outside the park and your pasturage is very dry and does not supply adequate enough food for your herd.

'With this said, I can assure you that you can bring your herd where the grasses are green, beside the River Mara in the park, and graze freely without any fear of being attacked by any animals. We respect all the creatures—they are creatures of God—and are therefore our brothers and sisters.'

The Maasai leader considered this and then responded. 'We are honoured and privileged to attend your committee meeting. We have full support for your good cause. We would certainly like to discuss what you have said with our members. We should return to our village and will then inform you of our decision soon.'

There was a lot of other discussion, with Mr President then summarising the discussion and thanking the delegates for their support and cooperation. The meeting was then declared closed.

The date for next meeting with Mr O'Dingo, the Maasai leader, and his committee delegates was provisionally scheduled for Saturday December 4, 2010.

The Maasai leader informed the president that they would go back to their village and discuss the day's meeting with their community. Very soon after, they stated, they would inform the animals association of their decision.

Mr Tembo, Miss Swala and Miss Coracias escorted the guests to their home. On the way, there was some conversation about the future of the park, its animals and the Maasai people.

Mr Amolo said, 'I recon it would be a very good idea to implement a joint action. I am excited about how the animals are planning to adopt an entertainment programme, etc.'

The Committee Meeting with the Maasai Leader

The Maasai leader said, 'Your president has a strong personality, and we are confident we will succeed in our mission. We will convey your message to our community and hopefully be with you.'

Chapter 8: The Maasai Community's Decision

The Maasai delegates went to their village and held a meeting the following day. They informed their community members of the discussion they had had with the Animals Association at the Maasai Mara Park the previous day. They informed the villagers that all the animals, birds and reptiles in the Maasai Mara National Park had formed an 'association in mind of stopping the safari jeeps from entering the park, as the tourists were disturbing the peace and tranquillity of the park and polluting and endangering their lives.

'They invite us to join them for the benefit of both communities.'

One Maasai villager called Kakenya said, 'We do not live in the park, nor are we animals. We live just outside the park and the safari jeeps are not causing any harm to us. Moreover, they come to see our village, to watch our dance and pay us. It is a source of income, so why should we stop them coming to our village? Why would we join the animals and create our own problem?'

Lekuton, another Maasai villager said, 'It's true they pay us but they do not pay enough for our dance. I feel they should pay us more or they shouldn't come to our village to insult us.' He also said, 'Do you know they laugh at our way of living, our diet, our homes? Isn't that an insult to us? They should learn our culture! They do not pay us directly but through the jeep driver and the middle man, who takes the money and gives us very little. I do not feel it's worth showing our village or our beautiful dance to them. Not at all.'

Olemelli, another distinguished Maasai villager, said, 'They are causing pollution, no doubt about it. They are scaring our herds and they laugh at our way of living. I feel they should pay more or they shouldn't come to our village at all.'

The leader of the delegate, Mr O'dingo, who had attended the Animals Associations meeting, said, 'When we three arrived for the meeting, their President, Mr Simba, and all the committee members received us politely and honourably.

They explained the problem they are facing from the visitors entering the park, and how we all could join with them to settle the problem for the benefit of both communities. I fully sympathise with their cause. If we join them, it will be beneficial to us also. What their president, Mr Simba, said to us, is that the Safari Park Authority has earned enormous sums of money from tourists in the past, and have done so for many years, but that they have directed very little of that towards the improvement of the park or to our benefit. Not a single shilling has come our way. It really should be their duty to look after our health and our welfare.

'Every point he made is very true. Look at our village and the environment in which we are living! There are no medical facilities for us! For any minor illness, we have to go to the city or die here without treatment! We need a hospital in our village.

'They also demand a veterinary hospital in the park and a vaccination programme for all the newborn animals. I was impressed upon hearing the speech of their president. He is very intelligent and considers everything well.'

'What is the president and who is their president?' Lemasolai, a tall, slim dancer of the Maasai asked.

'The president is the leader of the association. He is known as Mr Simba and is a dominant lion,' the Maasai leader explained.

'You have heard the plan of the Maasai Mara Animals Association, but now you must decide if you want to join them and form a united force to put pressure on the Safari Park Authority to meet our demands,' 'Mr O'Dingo, the Maasai leader, advised.

The majority voted yes and stated that they should join and demand that the authority make improvements to the park for the people's wellbeing.

Olekorinko, another villager, was doubtful whether there was a conspiracy behind the plan and asked, 'How can you trust a ferocious animal like a lion, or indeed a leopard or a cheetah and the others? It could be their plan to kill us!'

'Do you really think such an action would work? Did you carry any weapon?'

'Of course we did,' Amolo replied.

Mr Amolo, who had attending the meeting with Mr O'dingo, commented, 'No, that is not true. We can trust Mr Simba and his team. My heart was pounding uncomfortably before I went, but as soon as I saw the carnivorous and herbivorous animals sitting together, my heart calmed straight way. We had seen the ferocious animals, like the lion, cheetah and leopard, and many other herbivorous animals, such as the wildebeest, gazelle, birds and reptiles, all sat together and chatting amongst themselves. I did not understand their conversation but it was apparent that they were talking about the Safari Park Authority and the tourist activities in the park. They were laughing aloud without any fear. They are really very concerned about the future of the park.

'When you asked us to represent our community, I had a strange feeling that I might not come back alive. We took with us our swords hidden inside our dress, just in case they were to attack us. We wanted to be able to protect ourselves. But, to my surprise, that was not necessary at all. Have you ever seen or imagined two groups of animal, like the lion and leopard, being friendly with the zebra or gazelles?

'Now, it is happening here in the Maasai Mara Park,' Mr Amolo said. You will soon see: humans and animals are a part of one large community.

'What is more, Mr Tembo told us we don't need to carry any weapons. That we would be protected if necessary. We felt they are in one big family, which their president also confirmed to us. We settled down and the meeting started. I was looking suspiciously at all the animals around us and trying to understand their body language and smell out any danger. When the president spoke, my fear disappeared and I felt like I was instantly one of their friends. I held my weapon close to my chest under the clothing, just in case it was to fall out and I would end up humiliated!' He then continued, 'A meeting has been arranged with the Maasai Mara Animals Association for December 4, 2010. You decide whether you want to join them and, if so, who the delegates are that will represent us at the Animals Association.'

'I do not think we should join. It could be a trap for us. These carnivorous animals have a plan to take us there and kill us,' Mr Korinko, one of the less trusting Maasai villagers, said.

Mr O'dingo responded. 'As Mr Amolo told you, I was suspicious before I went there, but when I was introduced to their president and the other committee members, all my fears disappeared and I did not feel scared at all. We carried weapons with us for our protection, but that was unnecessary. In fact, we were surprised to see the carnivorous and herbivorous animals, the reptiles and birds all are friends, which is what we were told by them.

'You need to decide who should represent us and what our demands of the Safari Park Authority should be.'

It was decided in the meeting that Mr O'Dingo, Mr Amolo and Mr O'Ginga would represent the Maasai people in all future meetings as no other Maasai was seen to be willing to take the risk of going to the Animals Association meeting.

It was also decided that demands would include:

1. Medical facilities for the people (hospital);
2. Improvements should be made to the village;

3. Improvement should be made to the roads; and

4. There should be proper education (school) and a healthcare centre for all the children.

Chapter 9:
The Second Committee Meeting with the Maasai Leader

The second meeting with the Maasai delegates was held on December 4m 2010 in the Conference Arena located beside the River Mara. Under the beautiful umbrella Acacia tree, hundreds of weaver birds' nests hung from the branches, blowing back and forth like a pendulum in an isolated part of the safari park where no safari vehicles could disrupt the meeting.

Mr Tembo, Miss Swala and Miss Coracias escorted the Maasai delegates to the venue.

This part of the park was recognised as a favourite of Mr Simba; he would often venture there with his family, wanting to just relax and spend some time. He had even gone to the trouble of creating a second den.

When the time came, Mr Lion stepped into the role of the president and welcomed all the respectable delegates and his committee members.

The Second Committee Meeting with the Maasai Leader

He summarised the previous meeting's discussion and then requested that the Maasai delegates inform the committee of their decision regarding the plan.

The Maasai leader, Mr O'dingo, commented, 'Mr President, dear friends, it is my pleasure to inform you that we are proud to attend your meeting. I am impressed at seeing your enthusiasm, action for the good cause, the desire to make improvements to this land of ours. We are with you and we consider you as friends. You can expect our full-hearted support.'

An applaud erupted amongst the animals and people.

He then went on to state, 'We will work together and live together, and I am confident we will build a relationship living together, working together, eating together—and all without fear. We will build a safari park to be envied by everybody.'

Once again, everybody applauded.

'I feel the Safari Park Authority will not dare to ignore us,' he continued.

The president thanked the Maasai leader for their cooperation and said, 'Our next agenda is to write a letter to the Safari Park Authority.'

A letter was drafted:

The Second Committee Meeting with the Maasai Leader

The Maasai Mara Animals Association
Den No. 56
Pelewa Track
River Mara
Maasai Mara Safari Park
Kenya

December 4, 2010
Our reference: MMAA 001/DEC/2010

For the attention of the Maasai Mara Safari Park Authority:

Dear Sir,

With regret we are compelled to write this letter to you giving one week's notice to stop the safari jeeps from entering our homeland. These safari cars are polluting our land and endangering our health and life. They are disturbing the serenity, peace and tranquillity of the place. They are nothing but peeping Toms; we have tolerated them for so long but it has now come to the stage that we have decided to take necessary action against these safari cars. Unless you stop them with immediate effect, we will be forced to take necessary action.

We await a reply at your earliest convenience.

Yours Sincerely,
Mr Simba, President of the Maasai Mara Animals Association.

The Second Committee Meeting with the Maasai Leader

One week passed without a reply or acknowledgement from the Safari Park Authority, despite the letter being delivered by hand. Mr Simba asked Mr Tembo whether anything had been received from the Safari Park Authority.

'I'm sorry to tell you that there has been nothing whatsoever.'

Mr O'Dingo discussed that a reminder letter be sent. A second letter was then drafted, utilising stronger language that threatened the authority that necessary action would be taken if the authority failed to comply with the contents of the letter.

The Safari Park Authority could hardly believe the letter was real. For the last fifty years, nothing like this had happened. Why now, suddenly, was there this change in animal behaviour?

'This must be a long-standing plan by the animals and the Maasai people.' Mr Thomas had a feeling that this sudden rebellious behaviour had been influenced by some external factors, and therefore needing thorough investigation. He called a committee meeting and discussed amongst his colleagues, and decided that the letter should be completely ignored. Mr Thomas made up his mind and said, 'I am sure this agitation and temporary emotional excitement will be settled. I am not going to be carried out by this threat. I have no intention of replying to this letter,' and with that he tore it up and put the letter in the bin.

'I personally feel that we should not agitate the animals, and that we should calm the situation and engage in dialogue with them,' suggested Miss Tana to Mr Thomas. 'Don't you think so, too? We should engage in dialogue with them and handle the situation peacefully. Of course, you are in charge of the park and it is your decision, however.' She then turned to the other committee members. 'What do you feel?'

Mr Thomas was adamant the threat should be ignored.

No reply was given.

The Second Committee Meeting with the Maasai Leader

The Maasai Mara Animals Association
Den No. 56
Pelewa Track
River Mara
Maasai Mara Safari Park
Kenya

December 10, 2010
Our reference: MMAA 002/DEC/2010

For the attention of the Maasai Mara Safari Park Authority:

Dear Sir,
With regret, we inform you that we have not received any rely to our previous letter dated December 4, 2010.

It seems you are not interested in talking to us regarding the problem we are now facing on a daily basis.

This is a reminder and ultimatum to you. Failure to take any action, on your part, will mean we will be compelled to take direct action against the safari tourists. We do not want to harm anyone, but the choice is yours.

Yours Sincerely,
Mr L Simba

Upon receiving the second letter from Mr Simba, Mr Thomas looked more concerned. He was restless, walking from one corner of his room to another, and frequently putting his hand to his forehead. He wiped his spectacles and put them back on his eyes, reading the letter again.

He could not take any firm decision himself. He decided to discuss this matter with his colleague—and to do so without delay. He asked Miss Tana to call all of his colleagues to his room.

He was dreaming more and more about the situation and how this could be resolved—a crisis that had been created by his own foolishness, his own short-sighted attitude.

He said to his colleague, 'We've received another letter and a warning from the Animals Association, presenting a direct threat of action against the tourists unless their demands are wholly fulfilled. I must admit I'm surprised to see this sort of animal behaviour. I personally feel we should not bow down to the animals...

'I just don't know... What should I do about this threat?'

The Second Committee Meeting with the Maasai Leader

'Well, I expressed my views the last time we spoke of this and how best we could resolve the dispute in a peaceful manner. I personally feel we should meet them and listen to their demands and try to solve things without an altercation,' said Miss Tana.

Another colleague, Steve, added his own input: 'We trained the elephant to do hard work. We trained horses and dogs, and went on to use them for our benefit. We trained ferocious carnivorous animals—the lion and the tiger—and used them in the circus. Now, suddenly, they have become intelligent and educated. They didn't go to school or college, so where have they gained so many clever ideas?

'The answer is simple, I feel. The Maasai people are behind these agitations. We should talk to them secretly and defuse the tension.'

'Do you think we should talk to the Animals Association or the Maasai leader to bring this problem to an end?' asked Mr Thomas.

Steve was glad that Mr Thomas had taken his view into consideration and was not encourage any such type of animal behaviour. If they bowed down to the animals, the demands would increase over time, and they would be expected to fulfil more and more. Not to mention other safari parks in Kenya would then end of full of animals making demands similar to those in this case.

'The whole country depends on safari tourism,' stated Mr Thomas. 'This will have an enormous effect on our economy and on the tourism industry.'

Mr Thomas received moral support from other colleagues and decided that he would ignore this letter also.

He asked all the safari car drivers to remain vigilant and to make note of any illegal or unusual behaviour from the animals or the Maasai people, and that if the humans were seen to be involved in any meetings with the animals, this was to be reported to the Safari Park Authority immediately.'

The following day, a wealth of information came arrived at the safari park office. A group of elephants had been seen moving from one part of the park to another, as reported by one of the drivers.

The Second Committee Meeting with the Maasai Leader

And then there was a large group of wildebeest, which had been going towards the south, and there was a lion, lioness and many other carnivorous animals following them all, 'possibly heading to some kind of meeting,' reported Paul, another jeep driver.

A flood of information reached the Safari Park Authority but none of it was particularly useful.

Again, more than two weeks had passed and no acknowledgement or reply to the letter was received by the association, though both the letters had been delivered personally.

Everybody thought they would receive a reply from the Safari Park Authority, but a response never came.

Chapter 10:
A Meeting for the Letters Sent to the Safari Park Authority

Mr Simba called an emergency joint committee meeting with the Maasai leaders to discuss the possibility of direct action against the Safari Park Authority due to their decision to ignore the two letters. Both had been delivered to them personally, yet no reply had been received.

Mr Simba said, 'I don't think our letter made any impression on the Safari Park Authority's decision not to reply. They chose to completely ignore us, thinking we are animals, and therefore unintelligent, helpless and powerless. It is now the right time to show them that we are *not* weak and we can take action!'

Kifaru commented, 'We must ensure proper planning in regards how we can take direct action when the safari cars approach the park. We need to inform all our members to be present for direct action and that they need to follow the instructions of the leader. A poorly outlined plan of action might jeopardise our whole mission.'

Mr Tembo nodded his head thoughtfully. 'We are not attacking the people inside the safari cars. That is a no.' He shook his head. 'Our aim is to pass the message to the Safari Park Authority that they cannot just ignore our letters, thinking of us as helpless and unable to do any harm. Our aim is to frighten the tourists and damage the safari jeeps without causing any physical harm to the humans.'

Mr Chui was listening quietly, holding his tongue. It was not uncommon for him not to speak much during the committee meetings. He opened his mouth and frightened some of the herbivorous animals, stating that, 'When we besiege the cars, they will obviously be frightened and will call the rangers. You know very well that the rangers carry guns. I am sure they would not hesitate to fire at us!'

Mr Simba looked at Mr Chui and asked seriously, 'Are you scared, Mr Chui?'

Mr Chui replied politely. 'Surely not, Mr President. I am not scared for my life, but I do not want any innocent animals to die.'

Mr Tembo added, 'We will be there in the thousands and they will be only a few. They will not be even a hundred. Moreover, the rangers will carry only a few guns and they will be few in number. I feel they might try to scare us by firing into the air. Also, by the time the rangers come, our action of besieging the cars, damaging them and frightening the tourists will be done with, and we can then disperse before the rangers arrive. I feel they will be scared of us, and we should not be scared of them.'

'They cannot kill us right and left. There is an Animal Rights Organisation, which will definitely take action against the Safari Park Authority if they fire at us,' commented Mr O'Dingo. 'There are various other organisations, such as the Animal Welfare group also. When the whole world comes to know that the safari people have slaughtered us right and left, tourists will stop coming to the park and the reputation of the Maasai Mara Safari Park will be severely damaged if not lost altogether. Even the park might be closed for good or even for a long time.'

A Meeting for the Letters Sent to the Safari Park Authority

Mr Simba was listening attentively, and then said, 'Maasai people are human and they might feel insulted by lions remark. We will besiege the cars in a different location by different groups of animal. We will block all the exit tracks so that no car can escape the park before our mission is complete. Please remember: each group will have a leader, and all the animals will follow their leaders' instructions. At 11am, we will disperse from the area.

'We need to be brave and strong when it comes to taking action against the Park Authority. I have no idea what is on their minds, and so we need to be open to anything. Now is the time for direct action.

'All the animals will need to gather around the safari jeeps. I must make it clear to you that nobody will attack any tourists inside the cars. Not under any circumstance. They are our friends and not foe, and we should not target them.

Mr Simba then requested that the Maasai leader inform his community about the action and ask them to join in a large number to show support.

Mr Simba then asked the eagle to communicate the message from the sky to every resident in the park.

The following morning, when the safari jeeps had arrived in the park according to the plan of Mr Simba, a few animals went very close to one of the cars in one part of the park. In another part of the park, Mr Duma took the lead. Mr O'Dingo led another group of animals to another area in the park. Some other animals and the Maasai people took the lead in another direction.

People inside the cars were amazed to see the lions, elephants and other animals so close. They took photographs, and expressed amazement that they had been able to take photographs of carnivorous animals. They informed the other safari cars of what they could see and, in no time, a large number of safari jeeps appeared.

More and more animals started to arrive at the spot. In time, it was not only carnivorous animals but also herbivorous animals, birds and reptiles that were present at the spot. The Maasai people were also present. The tourists were puzzled to see humans and animals together in the park, all roaming like people in big cities from different countries and different cultural backgrounds, and all friendly with one another.

Lion cubs were watching the fun from a distance, hiding in the grassland, playing with their mother. Animals surrounded the safari cars from every angle.

The safari cars were besieged for more than an hour. There was no escape route for the safari cars and so they could not return to their lodge. The elephants rubbed their bodies across the cars and damaged the vehicles. Seeing the elder ones rubbing their thick skin across the car, a teenage elephant, Gamba, decided he would sit on the bonnet of one of the jeeps. Very quickly, the bonnet collapsed and he almost fell, but luckily his father was close by to lend him his trunk and save him from falling.

As Gamba had sat on the bonnet, the back of the hood was lifted into the air. Everybody inside the car and many animals outside screamed. Upon hearing the commotion, many other animals, namely Miss Swala Pala, Miss Gazelle and a singing bird came rushing to Gamba. They had known Master Gamba since the friendship movement had begun a few weeks before. Master Gamba was known to be strong, handsome and caring. Moreover, Master Gamba's father, Mr Tembo, was the leader of the friendship movement.

They had been planning to form a dance group called 'Dance & Dance', and Master Gamba had been assigned the leader. Now, they were concerned for their leader.

They asked, 'Are you alright?' He replied, 'I am fine. I thought it was a good place to sit on but I didn't realise the safari jeeps are so fragile! If I push, it would probably go right into that ditch!'

They all giggled as they looked on at the condition of the safari jeep's bonnet.

~*~*~*~

A Meeting for the Letters Sent to the Safari Park Authority

At another point in the day, a singing bird composed a song and began to sing in a nearby tree. She was beautiful, her voice melodious. Mr Gamba, Miss Swala Pala, Miss Gazelle, other animals and a dancing bird called Jacksons Widow Bird began to dance. Even the people inside the cars forgot their miseries and enjoyed the music.

Once the song and dance were over, there was a big applause for the singer and the dancers. They asked the tourist to come out of their car and enjoy the dance, but they were too frightened to leave. The elephant said to them, 'We are friends. You can come out of the car without any fear. We are not going to harm you. You can walk freely and return to your lodge.'

The safari jeep drivers did not allow any tourists to leave the cars or even lower the glass window. One rhino came running and head-butted the side of a different safari jeep. One side of the car was badly dented, and it was even pushed a few feet away into the distance, with the rhino's horn stuck into its metal. He was pulling and pushing to release his horn from the body of the jeep, but to no avail.

When the rhino was trying to pull his horn from the jeep's body, pulling and pushing, the whole car was being tossed around like a ship in a stormy sea. Other animals also assisted him but without any success. Finally, he was rescued by an elephant. He thanked everybody, especially the elephant. All the animals laughed upon seeing the condition of the car.

The gazelle and other antelopes punctured the tyres of all the cars, damaging the cars to the point they could not move an inch from the place. All the people in the cars were severely shaken and frightened. Their joy, pleasure and happiness disappeared in no time, like it had never been there at all.

The lion asked the Maasai people to tell the tourists that they could leave the safari jeeps without fear, that no animal would harm them.

'We all are friends.'

But the drivers prevented any tourist from leaving the car due to the big risk of leaving. They then had to make the decision to call the rangers to disperse the animals and rescue all the tourists traveling in their cars. When the rangers arrived, most of the animals had already left.

A similar incident happened in every corner of the park. Some of the Maasai people became very friendly to the car drivers and engaged in long conversations with them. The purpose for the besiege was discussed with them; the travellers were assured that they were safe and that no harm would be come to them. The Maasai people further advised that they could leave their cars if they wished to do so; however, the safari car drivers did not want to take the risk by allowing them to get out of their cars.

The tourists requested that the Maasai people stand amongst the animals to have a group photo, which would be unique. The group photo with the various carnivorous, herbivorous animals, birds, reptiles and Maasai people was at first: nobody had ever had such a photo taken before.

The news spread like wildfire across all the other parks and to all over Kenya and beyond, with the rumour whispering that the animals had attacked the safari jeeps.

That evening, no safari cars were seen in the park, and the animals were happy. The following morning, newspapers printed colour photographs of the animals besieging the safari jeeps, as well as pictures of the damaged cars. Only a handful of the safari cars were seen to be far away, watching the animals with their binoculars, choosing not to take the risk of coming closer and instead watching the animals from a far distance. Most of the animals were hiding in the grassland and bushes so that the tourist could not see them. They were not prepared to come very close to the animals' dens. The number of safari cars coming to the park had greatly reduced.

The Safari Park Authority had received the message.

Bewildered, Mr Thomas tried to contact the Maasai Mara Animals Association urgently and called an urgent meeting with his colleague to discuss how to handle the situation.

The very same day, a letter came from the authority, which had been long expected, asking the Animals Association not to take any further action and seeking out direct discussion. A date

A Meeting for the Letters Sent to the Safari Park Authority

was given for a proposed meeting, but the date—March 2011—was three months later. In the meantime, the Safari Park Authority started enquiring why, all of a sudden, the animals' behaviours had changed.

'Who was the Brain Child behind this problem?' they questioned. 'How can we stop these movements?'

They tried to separate the Maasai people from the Animals Association by threatening some of the members and bribing others to break the organisation's 'unity and strength'. Mr Simba got the message and called a committee meeting with Mr O' Dingo, the Maasai leader.

Mr Simba addressed the meeting and said, 'Dear friends, we have today received a letter from the Safari Park Authority, but they are just buying time—most likely to find out who is behind the problem and how they can create a rift amongst us in order to break our unity in solving this problem. Their policy is to divide and rule. We need to be very careful, and of course we should not put our feet in their traps.

'Three months' notice is too long; we want immediate action and an imminent solution.'

Another strong letter was sent to the Maasai Mara Safari Park Authority, mentioning the need for an immediate solution, with failure to do so meaning the Animals Association would be compelled to take further 'more severe action'.

The letter was posted in time. Now had a proper address from the letter sent to them by the park authority. After receiving a strong and threatening letter from the Animals Association, the Safari Park Authority replied promptly. They stated that they were willing to have a meeting with the Animals Association but not with the Maasai people owing to the fact that the name of the organisation was Maasai Mara Animals Association.

Mr Simba took his time to consider things and then replied:

A MEETING FOR THE LETTERS SENT TO THE SAFARI PARK AUTHORITY

The Maasai Mara Animals Association
Den No. 56
Pelewa Track
River Mara
Maasai Mara Safari Park
Kenya

January 28, 2011
Our reference: MMAA 003/JAN/2011

For the attention of the Maasai Mara Safari Park Authority:

Dear Mr Thomas,
Thanks for your prompt reply. It seems you are not serious about the whole affair.

Whatever the name of the organisation, it includes Maasai people and all the animals, birds, reptiles and any creature of God, living in this park.

Yours Sincerely,
Mr Simba
President of Maasai Mara Animals Association

Maasai Mara Safari Park Authority
The Lodge of the Park
Maasai Mara
Kenya

February 2, 2011

Dear Mr Simba,
Thanks for your letter, Ref MMAA/003/Jan 2011, January 28, 2011.

Please note: a meeting will be held February 5, 2011, venue The Lodge of the park at 9AM. Please confirm the date is acceptable to you, as well as the number of delegates attending the meeting for security arrangement.

Yours Sincerely,
Mr D. S. Thomas
Management of the Maasai Mara Safari Park

A MEETING FOR THE LETTERS SENT TO THE SAFARI PARK AUTHORITY

The Maasai Mara Animals Association
Den No. 56
Pelewa Track
River Mara
Maasai Mara Safari Park
Kenya

Dear Mr Thomas,

Thanks for the letter dated February 2, 2011.

This date for the meeting is acceptable to us. Please note the following members will attend the meeting: Mr Tembo, Mr Kifaru, Mr O'Dingo, Mr Amolo, Mr O'Ginga and myself.

Yours Sincerely,
Mr Simba
President of Maasai Mara Animals Association

Chapter 11:
The Meeting With the Safari Park Authority

The Maasai People had a separate meeting with their community with the aim of discussing in detail their demand to be put forward to the Safari Park Authority in collaboration with the Animals Association on February 5, 2011.

Kakenya, a Maasai villager, suggested, that they had a golden opportunity to put their demands to the park authority and accordingly achieve maximum influence on their benefit.

'Our request for the improvement has previously been ignored by the Park Authority,' he stated. 'Now we will see how they ignored our joint action. I can't see what's going to block us from joint action against the Authority.'

'This cannot wait!' said Korinko, another senior villager recognised as having some authority in his community. 'I must remind you that we should put forward some more new demands besides the old ones. We need to look after each other and help each other, don't we?'

In one voice, everybody agreed. 'Yes!'

Meitikini said to all the villagers, 'Do you know, a new in-charge has arrived whose name is Mr Thomas. He is a nice and polite gentleman. He is not at all rude or stubborn like Mr Frank.' He took a pause for a moment and then said, 'If the animals are willing to be friendly with us, then I think we should be friendly to them.'

We have already discussed in our previous meeting what our demands will be, and we will not back down from these,' said Mrs Namunyak. 'However, it will not be an easy job. But nonetheless, I believe we can achieve this.' Namunyak could smell a new determination amongst the Maasai people to achieve their long-deserved rights.

As planned, the meeting took place on February 5, 2011. Mr Simba, Mr Tembo, Mr Kifaru, Mr O'Dingo and two Maasai delegates attended the meeting.

Mr Simba and his team were surprised to see the security arrangement. Armed guards escorted them from the edge of the Maasai village to the venue. It was not the kind of venue that would allow delegates like Mr Simba and Mr Tembo to sit comfortably for a serious discussion. The venue was not at all well suited to large animals, such as Mr Tembo. Nonetheless, he somehow managed to enter into the room and pretend he was comfortable.

Mr Thomas welcomed all the delegates and asked them to be seated. He introduced the delegates to the members of his committee and then offered some drinks. He read the agenda for the meeting, which was centred on discussing the demands of the Maasai Mara Animals Association. He requested that Mr Simba put forward his demands.

Mr Simba addressed the committee. 'Mr Thomas, Committee members, dear friends, thank you for having us here today to discuss the problems we are facing due to the increased number of safari jeeps entering the park, and subsequently breaching the peace and tranquillity of the environment, and endangering the lives of the residents of the park. We are here today to discuss these issues and how best these can be resolved amicably.

'You raised an objection about the name of the organisation and wanted to exclude the Maasai people from our organisation, stating that they do not belong to the animal kingdom and that they do not live in the park, but just outside the park. This is not true. We are residents of the Maasai Mara. We all live by the side of the River Mara, and the Maasai people are our neighbours. If the name of the organisation is an obstacle to negotiation, we have no objection when it comes to changing the name. We feel that the most appropriate name would be the Maasai Mara Residents Association. I am sure you can't object to this change in name.'

The Maasai leader explained Mr President's message to the committee in simple English.

Mr Thomas agreed to the proposal.

Mr Simba then went on to say, 'Perhaps you may be aware: every morning and evening, safari jeeps bring visitors to the park, which has been going on for more than fifty years. Initially, only a few jeeps would come, but gradually, over time, the number has increased, and now it has reached a point that is unacceptable to us. I am sure the number will continue to increase up and up. Sometimes, ten or even fifteen jeeps come and disturb us! They look for us everywhere. There is no hiding place!'

When Mr Simba was addressing the committee, Mr Thomas and his committee members were trying to read the body language of all the animals sitting with them in the meeting.

Mr Simba further stated, 'You know very well that, if visiting anybody's house, you need their permission. Here you are not visiting us but you are invading our dens. You call us animals—fine, we never objected to that—but that does not mean we haven't got a heart, we haven't got feelings. When we are hurt, we feel pain just like you. Tears fall from our eyes. We need to eat drink and sleep—just like you. You may be aware that we rest and sleep in the morning after hard work in the dusk and in the dawn. You live with your families in beautiful, comfortable, air-conditioned houses, enjoy good food and sleep at night in a comfortable bed. Look at us: we sleep in grasslands in the cold, in the wind and in the rain. We do not sleep in comfortable beds but rather in hostile environments, and we need proper rest. We live in fear of being attacked by other animals.

We go to sleep in the mornings and safari jeeps disturb us. These vehicles break our serenity and the tranquillity of the park. And not to mention the jeep engines pollute the environment. We are having difficulty breathing, and our babies and children suffer from breathing problems. As a result, they are getting weaker, and they are not as strong as we are due to inhaling polluted air and living in a hostile environment. They cannot run fast, nor can they catch their prey as well as the older generations. A lot of them are dying from hunger and diseases. They are experiencing a premature death. If we allow this to continue, very soon after, you will see no animals in the safari park.

'We want all of this to stop immediately. More recently, we had an incident when a safari jeep almost ran one of our close friends over when he was sleeping! Tell me, how is this acceptable?'

Mr Simba gave a very emotional presentation that touched everybody's heart.

Mr Thomas responded. 'I am sorry to hear of these incidents. Thank you for bringing this to our attention and for highlighting the problem you are facing. You have opened my eyes—I never thought this issue was running so deep. I have noted your points. And now I must conclude by saying that appropriate measures will be taken to prevent such incidents from happening again.

'As an example, I will instruct the safari jeeps to drive only on the track and avoid densely populated areas. You want to change the name of your organisation to the Maasai Mara Residences Association, which is acceptable to us. I must point it out, however, that you are not a registered organisation. And with this noted, for future negotiations, you must register your organisation and must have a written constitution.'

'We do have a written constitution,' Mr O'Dingo clarified. 'Here is a copy for your attention, Mr Thomas,' he stated.

Mr Thomas said, 'Thank you, Mr President. So far, I have understood your first problem as being safari cars visiting the park in the morning, which is not acceptable to you, and you want your visiting times to be rescheduled.'

Mr Simba and the other committee members nodded their heads and said, 'Yes.'

'We can arrange an alternative time, convenient to you,' offered Mr Thomas.

'The second problem of the jeeps' diesel engines polluting the environment can also be solved by having cars with different fuel or even electric or solar power ones. This can be arranged, though it will take some time as we would need to order new vehicles.

'We agree on these two points and arrangements will be put in place in time. I am confident you now won't disrupt the safari trips any further?'

Mr Simba' said, 'Thank you for the offer, but that's not all we are demanding for, nor have we come here for discussion. There are other important issues to be considered.

As a first point, when considering the visitors the Safari Park Authority has brought in over the years, and the profit that has generated, how much money has been invested in park improvement? Not a single shilling! How much have you spent on the Maasai people or on us? Not much! Don't you feel you have an obligation to improve the health and wellbeing of the Maasai people and the animals? Look at the conditions in which the Maasai people are living! Look at our conditions! Look how all of us are living! Look at the condition of the roads!'

Mr Thomas shook his head. 'I can't agree on this. We spend large sums of money on improving the park every year. It is a large area and it costs a lot to ensure maintenance. I agree it needs improvement, but I cannot agree that we have not made any investments in this direction,' Mr Thomas replied.

The Maasai leader, Mr O'Dingo responded. 'I cannot see any improvement or maintenance you have carried out in our homeland during the last few years. I have lived in this park for the last twenty years. I have not noticed any change, but rather exactly the same conditions over the last many years!

The Meeting with the Safari Park Authority

'Look at the roads! I must appreciate the patience of the tourists traveling through such horrible roads to see us!'

'Now, what improvements are you looking for exactly? What improvements should have been done?' asked Mr Thomas.

'We have written to you previously about the necessary improvements, but unfortunately, till today, we have not received any response,' said Mr Amolo. 'If you are concerned about us, you should have replied to our demands and discussed things with us,' said Mr Amolo.

'We want medical facilities for the Maasai people, a local hospital and free medical treatment for everybody. Not to mention a veterinary hospital for the animals. Our babies—both human and animal—are dying from various diseases, and so we also need a vaccination programme for the babies,' said, Mr O'Dingo.

'Before you were in charge of the park, the Maasai people sent a few petitions regarding our problems, seeking out a solution; however, all our petitions were ignored by the Park Authority.'

Mr Thomas replied, 'I am sympathetic to your good cause, and I am sure we will find a solution.'

'Moreover, we want our animals from needing to kill any other creature in this park. All the animals are our brothers and sisters, and the Maasai people are also our brothers and sisters. We are all creatures of God and, in His eyes, we are all equal. There is no discrimination. We are His sons and daughters, and so we are brothers and sisters,' Mr Simba said.

'If you want the safari cars to come to this park,' he continued, 'then we will need a regular supply of food, gifted by the Safari Park Authority.'

Mr Thomas's temper rose to the surface. Confused beyond measure, he asked in a perplexed voice, 'What?'' He was shocked and in disbelief. 'You want us to supply your food? We haven't caged you! You are free in the park! You are capable of hunting food for yourselves! We haven't stopped any of that! Have you gone crazy?

'Your other demands can be considered, but your last demand—to have your food supplied everyday by us—is absolutely not acceptable to me, nor to my committee. Do you have any idea how much it would cost to supply food to all of you, every single day? Do you know how many carnivorous animals there are in this park?'

'You must have the list. According to our counting, it is just under six hundred,' Mr O'Dingo contributed.

'It is a huge expenditure, and the safari park authority cannot afford it,' Mr Thomas declared.

'You don't have to pay from your pocket,' Mr O'Dingo countered. 'Pass the buck to your client .'

'How?' Mr Thomas asked in surprise.

'You add surcharges and detail the reason for them, such as environment charges, Maasai Mara welfare charges, animal welfare charges, green charges, and so on. I am sure the tourists would not object to paying a few more shillings for the good of the animals and the park,' said Mr O'Dingo.

Mr Thomas replied, 'We cannot just increase the fair citing lame excuses like these! This is unjust to the tourist, and I am sure the number of visitors would decrease and our earnings would be affected!'

'I am sure the tourists won't mind paying a few more shillings for the environment and for the welfare of the Maasai people or for the better living conditions of the animals!' noted Mr O'Dingo. 'Moreover, we have a plan to entertain them when they are in the park.'

There were long discussions regarding the last demands of the Association. It was apparent that Mr Thomas and his committee members were having difficulties in understanding Mr Simba's accent. As such, Mr Simba asked Mr O'Dingo to communicate with Mr Thomas.

Mr Thomas said, 'If we provide food for you, it will then be detrimental to your health.'

Mr O'Dingo asked, 'How so?'

'If you get your food given to you on a plate, you won't be running to catch your prey, and so you won't do any exercise at all! That'll make you idle, lazy and inactive, and it wouldn't be good for you,' said Mr Thomas' 'Not to mention the fact you will grow fatty and die a premature death as a result of being obese!

'I request you to withdraw the last demand.'

'Well, Mr Thomas, perhaps you have forgotten that we live longer in captivity in the zoo when we are inactive. We die prematurely in the wilderness, through being injured, such as when trying to catch prey. We fight amongst ourselves for our territory.' countered Mr Simba.

Mr President, I am well aware of our statistics,' advised Mr Thomas. 'But still, what I wanted to convey to you is that regular exercise is good for your health.'

'You don't need to worry about that. We thought about all of this very carefully and we have a plan for that. I am sure you will earn ten times more if you accept our proposal and cooperate with us. It would be to your benefit also,' said Mr O'Dingo.

With his eyes wide in wonder, Mr Thomas asked, 'How?'

Mr O'Dingo replied, 'We have thought about this. We had a long discussion in one of our committee meetings and we have decided that we would have regular exercises. We had already planned to take part in various competitive sports. For example, the Maasai people will run with the lions, cheetahs, leopards and other animals and, as a result, their running skills will be much like the cheetah's, meaning their ability would improve and they would be able to compete in the Olympics and other competitive sports. I am sure they would earn more gold medals for our country! Other animals would also compete for various sports activities. The lion and other carnivorous animals could chase the zebra, gazelle, wildebeest and other animals. They would run for their lives. We would have marathons and long jump, and maybe even water polo matches with the elephants. Perhaps swimming competitions for the crocodiles.

'I list only few to you but we also have a long list of sports activities. Many other sports would entertain the safari park visitors and, as a result, our reputation will spread to other parks in Kenya and beyond.

'We are confident more visitors would then choose to visit our park. Though, I confess, I am worried whether you will be able to handle the flow of visitors. Do you have enough accommodation for them? Do you have enough cars? Can you pull together the manpower to manage such a big demand from tourists? If not, please look into this soon.

The Meeting with the Safari Park Authority

'When visitors visit the park, we would act as a predator catching a prey, but we would not harm anybody or kill anyone; rather, we would be just acting. Visitors would not be able to figure out that it is all an act and not real.

And then there will also be dance competitions by birds, and antelopes.'

Mr Thomas was speechless for a few minutes.

Mr O'Dingo said to Mr Thomas, 'We have already started the competition on a trial basis, and it is proving to be very popular amongst us, as well as in the animal kingdom. In fact, you are invited to come and watch whenever you like!'

Miss Tana, assistant to Mr Thomas, whispered something in the ear of Mr Thomas. He then stated, 'My assistant Miss Tana is impressed with your plans. She is optimistic about the plan. And although she thinks it is a fantasy story, she recognises that, with good planning and good leadership, it could work.'

Mr President became very angry, and so Mr Tembo, Mr O'Dingo and other animal delegates strongly objected to the remark made by Miss Tana and demanded an apology.

She said, 'My intention was not to question Mr President's authority or your plan, but what I wanted to say was that good leadership is required to have a project like this. I am sorry if I have inadvertently offended anyone or indeed the members of the organisation. I sincerely apologise to you, Mr President, for any misunderstanding. I withdrew my comment.'

Mr Thomas could not say another word; they were all looking at him. He muttered that, in theory, it is a brilliant idea but that, from a practical standpoint, it might be difficult to carry out.

Mr O'Dingo then asked, 'Mr Thomas, did you say something?'

Mr Thomas replied, 'Yes, what I am saying is we will consider your proposal. It was a very fruitful discussion and I will write to you very soon.' Mr Thomas then asked if there was anything else left to discuss.

Nobody asked any more questions and Mr Thomas said, 'I declare the meeting closed for today.'

Mr Simba then said, 'If there are any further clarifications required in regards our proposal, please contact me without hesitation. We want an amicable, peaceful settlement, and I am sure you also want this to be agreed upon very soon.'

Mr Thomas thanked all the delegates and declared the meeting closed.

The next meeting was scheduled to be held on February 15, 2011, 10AM. Mr Simba requested that the next meeting be held beside the River Mara under the blue sky and the umbrella acacia tree in the middle of nature.

'This will give you an experience as to how we live in our environment,' he stated.

Mr Thomas agreed.

'In which case, I think we have presented our demands well,' Mr Simba said.

Mr Thomas then escorted Mr President, Mr O'Dingo and the other delegates to their destination.

Chapter 12:
The Extraordinary General Meeting

Mr President called an extraordinary general meeting to inform the general members about the outcome of the meeting with the Safari Park Authority the previous week. The meeting was necessary as all the animals were eager to know the outcome of the meeting, which Mr Lion recognised would help in gaining the general public's confidence and increasing their morale and support for the committee.

Mr President welcomed all the members and thanked them for attending. He opened by saying, 'I am glad to inform you that we were involved in some tough negotiations with the Safari Park Authority, with several letters of correspondence passing both ways, and then a face-to-face meeting. Initially, they refused to recognise us as an organisation, mentioning it was not properly constituted. They also tried to divide us,

The Extraordinary General Meeting

emphasising the name Maasai Mara Animals Association as not being inclusive of the Maasai people due to them not being animals. Fortunately, they finally accepted us as an organisation when we proposed to have the organisation's name changed to Maasai Mara Residents Association and showed them our constitution.

Do you agree on the new name of our organisation, which from this point forward should be called the Maasai Mara Residents Association?

Almost everybody was in agreement, stating no objection to any such changes. It was accepted by the general members.

'I am sure we have presented our case very well. We convinced them how they would benefit from our proposal and earn more money than before our plan. We also stated why they should provide us with various facilities, which are our fundamental rights.

'I have also mentioned to you in the past that we are all friends and that no carnivorous animal would kill any other animal for a living. Some of you asked me if carnivorous animals would eat grass for a living. I also proposed to them that our food be provided by the Safari Park Authority so as to allow us not to kill any animal. In such a case, we all would live like a big family, as relatives and friends.' A big applaud sounded for the president and the committee.

'Three cheers for our president!' came the cries from every corner. Herbivorous animals shouted in joy, 'Long live our president!'

Mr President said, 'Once the Safari Park Authority accepts our proposal, we will then live together, as friends and in harmony and peace, in this tranquil land of ours under the acacia tree. We will enjoy sports and recreational facilities in the park. Birds will sing in the trees. We will swim in the River Mara like fish, without any fear of being attacked by crocodiles. The whole Maasai Mara Park will be like a dreamland. We will entertain visitors. The Safari Park authority will benefit and will earn more money than before. Our accounts department needs to work hard to keep an accurate record of all the safari cars and the number of people visiting the park so that the authority cannot deceive us and so as to ensure we get the right amount of food.'

Some of the herbivorous animals said, 'I am sure you will get your food from the Safari Park Authority, but how can you change your behaviour? It is your instinct to attack us when you see us isolated from the group, not to mention those who are infirm and children.'

Mr Lion said, 'You have raised a very valid point. The changes we are planning cannot come over night. It might take some time. Initially, there might be some incidents where some herbivorous animals are being attacked by others, but again the punishment for such a crime will be very severe. Please pass this message to the other animals. They must think twice before they attack any other animal.

'As stated, change will take time.'

A question was raised by a wildebeest. 'If we were to be killed or injured by an animal, how will you catch the criminal? How would you punish the perpetrator? And what sort of compensation will be given to the victims?'

'We would require a witness,' Mr President explained. 'There will be a committee who will look after the welfare of the animals. Any complaints will be the responsibility of the committee to judge and punish the criminal as they see it. Every animal should be vigilant. If anybody breaks the rules, please inform us and we will investigate and do what is necessary to hold the culprit accountable.' He then said specifically to the wildebeest, 'You are a large animal and you have two powerful horns. You graze in large groups. So why then are you so scared of any carnivorous animal? You must stand and protect yourself! If you stand firm and face the attacker, I am sure the attacker will be scared of you. Moreover, you can always graze in a group, and then there will be no question of you being scared of any other animal. You can attack carnivorous animals. Other animals would be scared of you if you are in a large group.'

'Very interesting,' commented the wildebeest. 'We never thought about this before.'

Many carnivorous animals were not happy with Mr Lion's remark; they felt that the lion had hurt their pride and damaged their image in front of the herbivorous animals. After all, the carnivorous animal had considered themselves to be superior to any other animal living in the park, and they thought they should dominate the park.

'Now we are friends, we are equals. We cannot have a friendship if you feel you are superior and look down on others,' Mr Simba further stated. 'I will advise all animals to stand together and face attackers, and I am sure nobody will then dare attack you if you stand united.'

It was then that a number of the animals asked, 'Why is it taking so long to have our food supplied by the Park Authority? How long do we have to wait for good news?'

Mr Simba replied, 'I know it is frustrating, but we must all be patient. We are winning, and the Safari Park Authority has recognised us as an organisation and are now having discussions with us. This is a step in the right direction! And as I have just mentioned to you, we have changed the name of the organisation to the Maasai Mara Residents Association, and so I need us to reorganise our committee members. All the elected committee members will remain in their position, with alterations only necessary as the Maasai leader is a very important partner; without their help and support, we would not be able to go forward. We would not be able to negotiate with the Safari Park Authority. As such, I propose that the Maasai leader be our General Secretary and Mr Tembo Assistant General Secretary. I have already discussed this with Mr Tembo and Mr Twiga, and they both agree this change is in the best interests of our organisation. The proposal also suggests Mr Twiga as a valuable member on the committee.'

Mr Twiga said, 'I have no objection, Mr President.'

Everybody accepted the change with an open heart.

Mr Simba then continued, 'I am eagerly waiting for a letter of confirmation from the Safari Park Authority to echo that they have accepted our proposal in principle. Very soon we will have our next meeting to discuss how these actions should be implemented. Nonetheless, we have a long way to go. So, friends, please have some patience and then we will be able to succeed.

'I would also like to remind you that any animal on the way to attend our committee meeting or general body meeting should not be attacked by any other animal. One very shameful incident happened on November 3, 2010, when one of our committee members was on her way to our meeting and was attacked by a large cat. She was chased her and, as a result, fell into the river and could not attend the meeting on time. This is a very shameful incident and I trust that this incident will never happen again. We have issued badges to all our committee members; they must wear these when they are on their way to attend our meetings. They should not misuse the badges by wearing them at any other time.

'I must thank you for your patience, cooperation and support. I am grateful to you all.'

The meeting was declared closed.

Mr President reminded everybody that they had two hours to get back to their home. He also stated that he would inform everyone of any new developments in the future, and thanked each member for their attendance.

Chapter 13:
The Draft Contract

The meeting took place with the Park authority on February 15, 2011, located in the open space under the umbrella acacia tree beside the River Mara and in a tranquil atmosphere. It was another beautiful day, one for enjoying the sunshine with the animals in the middle of the safari park, which was very exciting for everyone.

Nobody had attended such an exciting meeting before. President Mr Simba, Mr Tembo and Mr Kifaru welcomed all the delegates into the entrance on the arena. There were three animals and three humans, all walking through the long corridor of the animal trek, surrounded by tall, dried grass on either side, and into the arena, where the meeting was set to take place. Other committee members were already waiting.

The trek was an ideal place for any ferocious animal to hide and wait for vulnerable prey. It was a long corridor, and the narrow passage was uneven for delegates coming into the arena.

Miss Tana looked nervous, her uneasiness more evident than usual. She could barely walk in her high-heeled shoes as she ventured through the animal trek. In fact, she almost twisted her foot a few times. She thought she should have worn boots rather than such shoes, and quite possibly long trousers instead of a short denim skirt.

While venturing through the corridor, Miss Tana noticed an ugly looking creature's eyes gazing at her. She could see only two glaring eyes; they winked at her. She couldn't identify the creature, but she was terrified.

She was certain she was not returning home alive.

She gathered her strength, acknowledging that she was not alone. She thought she would request Mr Tembo carry her on his back. 'I am sure he wouldn't refuse,' she said aloud to herself. Nonetheless, she recognised that it would be embarrassing for Mr Thomas and for her.

Miss Tana was in a bad mood, but she knew she only needed to walk a few more steps to reach the meeting place. There were animal droppings on the trek, and the smell was not of any kind of delight to her. She consoled herself that she was not alone, that Mr Lion and the other committee members—most specifically Mr Tembo—were all with her. She knew in her heart they would all protect her.

Under the acacia trees, a thick layer of hay had been laid to make the seat comfortable for the committee members and for the honourable delegates. Mr President asked everybody to be seated and then addressed the meeting.

The open meeting place under the sky was not overly good for what miss Tana had anticipated. She looked unhappy; she was used to living a comfortable life. She was not willing to sit on hay; 'It is dirty,' she thought to herself, and her beautiful clothing would be spoiled and would be in need of washing again. Moreover, she knew she could possibly end up carrying the deadly bovine germ home—and there was no known treatment for that.

She had read a lot on the internet about animals and the infectious diseases they carry. She was not at all happy about the venue for the day's meeting.

Mr Simba requested that Miss Tana sit, but she was reluctant. She said, 'I am quite comfortable standing, thank you, Mr President.'

Mr Thomas looked at her and indicated that she should sit. She sat down, unwillingly. Struggling to cover her exposed legs, she looked miserable and dissatisfied, which was apparent from her expression.

'Well, my friends,' Mr Thomas said with a smiling face, 'welcome.' He then discussed what had been negotiated in the previous meeting, and read what had been accepted by everybody without any questioning. He also said, 'A matter for today's discussion involves making an agreement between the Maasai Mara Residents Association and the Safari Park Authority regarding the demands made by the former's Mr Simba,' stated Mr Thomas. My committee looked at the proposal very carefully,' he continued, 'and subsequently decided to make a contract with you on a temporary basis—notably for three months—

as a trial period. If this is successful, the contract will then be extended for one year.'

Mr Simba asked in surprised voice, 'What do you mean, a three-month period? What will happen after the one-year period expiries?'

'The contact would be renewed annually,' clarified Mr Thomas. 'This contract can be cancelled by either party by giving one month's notice with a genuine reason. I have drafted a contract. Please read it carefully and then we can discuss the contents.'

A copy was given to each member, with everyone then asked to read it carefully. Everybody did so, and silence filled the space.

Contract

This legally binding contract was made between the Maasai Mara Safari Park Authority and the Maasai Mara Residences Association on the day of --------------------------- 2011

This contract is presented on a trial basis, notably spanning only three months. At the end of the three-month period, the Safari Park Authority will decide whether or not the project is viable. If the Safari Park Authority feels it is viable and affordable, the contract will then be continued and renewed annually. If the project is not viable, the deal will then discontinue.

1. *We will rearrange the visiting time for the safari park tourists, deciding on one that is convenient to the residents of the park. Visiting times will be between 10AM and 6PM.*
2. *We will open a veterinary hospital for the animals in the park and a vaccination programme will be implemented for the newborn babies, notably from January 2012.*
3. *We will provide free medical facilities for the Maasai people, located in their homeland. We will improve their village and living*

environment as a whole. The time for this will be negotiated at a later date.

'Now, let me be clear on this point first before we continue any further negotiations,' said the Maasai leader. 'A Later date could be six months, twelve months or even longer. I suggest this should be within six months.'

Mr Thomas continued.

4. *As from March 2, 2011 through to May 31, 2011, we will supply free food to all carnivorous animals at a rate of once a day for a trial period of three months. This will apply to those who are registered on our records.*

'What will happen to those who cannot register by March 1, 2011?' asked Mrs Mamba.

'Any registration following March 1, 2011 will mean a delay to their food supply for a week as we have to arrange food,' stated Mr Thomas.

He then continued.

The Draft Contract

> 5. *If this project is successful and affordable, the contract would then continue, but the contract will be renewable annually.*
>
> *This is a legally binding contract. Any party breaching this contract is liable for prosecution, at which point the contract will be invalid.*

Once everybody had read the contract, discussion then took place.

'In regards rearranging the time at which the safari cars can visit, if they come after 10AM and leave the park before 6PM, would you have any objections?' asked Mr Thomas.

'We would have some peace, undisturbed sleep and rest in the morning. They can travel the park only on the track designated for safari cars to drive. They will not be allowed to drive in densely populated areas or at our babies' and children's playgrounds.

'Furthermore, they can stay and watch us as long as they want, but they must leave before dusk,' stated Mr Simba.

This clause was accepted by all the committee members. There would be various No Driving

Zones for the safari cars, which would be marked as required.

'In the case that a safari car enters the restricted zone by mistake, they will be warned and politely requested to leave the area. I request you to inform the safari car drivers not to trespass,' Mr Simba said in an authoritative tone.

'Of course,' said Mr Thomas.

Mr Tembo then stated, 'We are grateful that you have decided to open a veterinary hospital and arrange a vaccination programme. This will be of great help to the animal kingdom. Although it should be noted that we need to know the plan in detail very soon.'

'Definitely. We will inform you in good time,' Mr Thomas said.

'I am grateful that you took the right decision to provide free medical treatment for the Maasai people in their homeland, but you failed to mention in the contract and reference to opening a hospital in our area and how long it might take to implement the contract, as well as what kind of medical facilities you will be providing? Mr O'Dingo asked. 'My second question also concerns the type of improvement in our living conditions you are planning?'

'At present, I cannot provide you with details about the plan. In the future, however, we will have further meetings regarding this issue and how the contract can be implemented.

'Regarding improvement, we will discuss this in detail in the future,' Mr Thomas confirmed. 'Moreover, in regards the supply of free food, this would be very costly. Still, I am not sure how this could be financed. In addition, I feel it would be damaging to your health.'

The Maasai leader asked, 'How it will be damaging to our health, Mr Thomas? Not only should you not worry about that, we also have a plan, which I have explained to you before. I do not wish to repeat myself,' he explained to Mr Thomas.

'Well,' Mr Thomas responded, 'what I wanted to say to you is that some form of physical exercise is necessary for good health. But I suppose if you have a plan, it is no longer my concern.'

Mr Thomas continued his speech and then said, 'I need the total number of carnivorous animals living in the park and the number of dens.

How many adults and how many children in each family? I need this information without delay in order to issue ration cards for each member of a family.'

Mr Simba asked, in surprise, 'Ration cards? Why would you need ration cards for us?'

'Well, without them, of course I would not know how much meat to supply for each family.'

'You mean to say we would get only limited supply of meat every day? I have five spouses and ten children and grandchildren, so how much food would I get?'

Mr Thomas responded in a soothing tone, 'Don't worry, Mr President. We have calculated from statistics and scientific research, with both stating that each adult lion eats approximately seven kilograms of meat a day whilst each female eats approximately five kilograms of meat every day. We are very generous we have decided we would supply six kilograms of meat to both male and female adults. As you know, Mr President, there are more lionesses than lions in the park, and so the supply of food will be adequate for every family. And each child will get three kilograms of meat every day.' He also said, 'The supplies, however, will not come every day, but more likely every two or three days.'

Mr Simba sighed. 'So you mean to say that I will get six kilograms of meat every two or three days? Do you want us to die in starvation?'

Mr Thomas said, 'No, Mr President. We are not cruel and we will not allow you to starve. If food is supplied every two days, you would get twice the amount, whereas if food was delivered every third day, you would then get three times as much food. Twelve kilograms for two days or, if it was supplied every three days, eighteen kilograms of meat per adult.'

'An everyday supply of food is difficult as we just don't have the resources,' 'Miss Tana' said to the lion.

'And how will you determine whether a cub is a cub or whether he is an adult?' the lion asked Mr Thomas. 'Consider for a moment that a cub at two years old could be an adult very quickly thereafter.'

Mr Thomas said, 'As you have pointed out very clearly, we have similar views. We would consider three years and above to be an adult and we would therefore supply food accordingly. For that, we need to know the age of the individual animals.'

Astonishingly, Mr Duma addressed Mr Thomas. 'You have mentioned the lions' food supply, What about other carnivorous animals? The cheetah, leopard, crocodile and others? How much food will they get?'

All the big cats would get similar amounts of food as your president. Other animals, such as the hyena, fox, jackels, wild dogs and others would get a lesser amount depending on their body size and food habits. We have got a list of food and the amount each animal eats per day, and we will supply accordingly,' confirmed Mr Thomas. He also assured the committee that no animal would ever go hungry. 'In order to supply food, I will need the accurate number of animals in each family and their dates of birth or age.'

Mr Simba looked to Mr Thomas in surprise. 'Does this mean we have to have ration cards issued by the Park Authority? You must surely appreciate that, in the past, we never had any food rationing and we never required a date of birth, so

The Draft Contract

the system of recording a date of birth does not exist! I can give you the approximate age of each animal and, in the future, could state that you can record the date of birth for any new arrival in the family for the vaccination programme.'

Mr Thomas assured the committee and said, 'Mr President, I did not mean that! Each family member must have a number.' He also said, 'If you want the trial period to start on March 1, 2011, I will need all the names and the age of each animal within a week to arrange a ration card to be sent to each member in the den. This is required only to supply the right amount of food to each den.'

'Where would we keep the ration card?' the Maasai leader asked. 'They don't have a secure place to keep it.' He also asked, 'Is it that, when food is supplied, each member needs to stand in a queue to collect their ration?'

'No, we will keep the card for you and we will supply the right amount of food to each den,' Mr Thomas replied. 'He also said, 'Supplies will be given out on Mondays, Wednesdays and Saturdays. Moreover, when the supplies come, the head of the family should make sure that nobody attacks the food distributor. If any of the food distributors are attacked or insulted by any animal, the food supply will be stopped and the contract will be invalid.'

'You must appreciate, Mr Thomas,' continued the lion, 'that we live on meat only and that we are not like you and eat other's food as well. I am sure you eat near enough a kilogram of meat every day, and so how can you expect us to eat only five kilos of meat every day?'

The Maasai leader spoke then and said, 'We live only on meat, blood and milk, and we eat nearly half a kilogram of meat every day—and how could you decide that six kilograms of meat will be enough for a big lion like our president? And not only that, but a growing lion needs more meat to eat for energy. I feel an adult and a growing carnivorous animal needs ten kilograms of meat every day and a child needs five kilograms of meat every day!'

'What 'Mr O'Dingo has said,' continued Mr Lion, 'is absolutely correct and correctly highlights that the rations you speak of fall below the amount of food we need, meaning our survival will be at risk! Furthermore, our members will not accept this!'

Mr Thomas then replied, 'As I explained to the committee, our statistics show that a lion like you, Mr President, eats a maximum of seven kilograms whilst the lionesses eat five kilograms of meat each day. This means that, per head, six kilograms of meat is adequate for a family like yours. You said that you have five lionesses in your den, so you will get five kilograms of extra meat per day! In addition, we don't eat a kilogram of meat every day, and I am sure the Maasai do not eat more than half a kilogram of meat every day!'

Mr Lion shook his head and realised it was time to move forward. 'Now, regarding the trial period of three months, I feel it is not enough time to achieve a proper assessment of the situation. I feel it needs a minimum of six months to assess the situation properly. Furthermore, it takes time to adjust the new way of life, and the message needs to be spread amongst the tourists.'

'Let's see for three months. If we feel it needs more time, it can then be extended,' suggested Mr Thomas.

Mr O'Dingo' said, 'If we are signing a legally binding contract, it should be properly worded. No loose wording or different meanings in the contract, and it should be simple language so that everybody can understand it. We need to show it to our legal advisors before signing. So, please draft a contract properly, including all amendments, and send it to us without delay. If needed, we will highlight any changes to be made and then send it to you for a final signing.'

Mr President thanked all the delegates and told Mr Thomas it had been a very fruitful meeting and that, very soon, they would meet here again, possibly on February 20, 2011 at the same venue. Mr President then asked Mr Thomas, 'How did you like the venue?'

'Amazing! I've never had any meeting like this before on a bright sunny day under the blue sky and umbrella acacia trees, with the cold breeze blowing in from the River Mara. The location was really amazing.'

Mr Simba smiled and then asked, 'Would you have any objections if we were to have our next meeting here?'

'No not at all! It would be a pleasure!'

Miss Tana then said to Mr Thomas in a low voice, 'I do not like this place. It is very dirty; unhealthy. How can you have a further meeting in this place?'

Mr Thomas replied to Miss Tana rather pityingly, 'Please keep quiet.'

Mr President asked again, 'Mr Thomas, did you feel scared or threatened at any point in time?'

'Not at any point,' Mr Thomas smiling.

Mr President declared the meeting closed with the date of the next meeting agreed as February 20, 2011.

Chapter 14:
Legal Advice

The draft letter was shown to the legal advisor, who pinpointed the need to incorporate a few additional clauses.

Clause number 6:

The Safari Park Authority cannot kill animals in the park or remove animals from the safari park to supply food to the animals who are their friends and relatives, nor can they kill animals to keep the number under control without prior discussion with the Maasai Mara Residents Association and achieving their approval.

Clause number 7:

The Safari Park Authority cannot take unilateral decisions regarding the future of the park, without prior consultation with the Maasai Mara Residences Association and achieving their approval.

Mr President called an urgent general meeting and explained to the general members the negotiation his committee had undertaken with the Safari Park Authority. He asked all carnivorous animals to submit their family members names and approximate age to the secretary without delay. Failure to adhere to this requirement would mean food supplies would be delayed.

The vultures and eagles asked, 'What would happen to our food supply?'

Mr President said, 'In the past you shared food with us so you would continue to share food with us just as you did then.'

They were not happy. The vulture said, 'Share food with you?!' He laughed a displeased laugh. 'Food that you couldn't or you wouldn't want to eat, you left for us to eat and clean the plate. Do you leave food for us willingly? Did you ever invite us to share your plate with you? No, we always fought to get our share of food from you! What you leave for us is nothing but bones, which we cannot chew!'

Mr Eagle then addressed his community of eagles, in their own mother tongue, telling them to remain quiet and not to argue with the lion. Every eagle listened to him and kept their beaks firmly shut. Discussion ensued amongst the carnivorous animals, with questions surrounding how and where they would provide the names and ages of each family members. Such a system had never existed in the past.

Each group of animals were discussing amongst themselves how they would provide all the information necessary to get their food supply from the authority in a timely manner.

Madam Tai added her own thoughts. 'We are not scavengers. We must hunt for our food just like you. What happens to our food supplied by the authority?'

The vulture became angry and asked the eagle, 'Do you mean to say we are scavengers? We also hunt for our food!'

'Did I mention your name? 'Did I mention that you are a scavenger?' Madam Tai responded in a loud voice. 'That is *your* interpretation.'

'Your comment points a finger at *us*,' the vulture responded.

An argument then broke out between the vulture and the eagle; it was very difficult to stop them from accusing each other. Mr President put a stop to the argument and asked them to behave like good neighbours and to be open to helping each other in times of need. 'Did you attend our last meeting or any previous meeting?' he asked them.

The eagles kept quiet, whilst the vulture replied, 'Yes.'

'Then why did you keep quiet in our previous meetings?' he asked. 'I had already negotiated with the authority and I can't go back and ask for more food. They might think I am not serious and that I'm playing with their weakness. The whole negotiation could fall apart. You will simply need to wait for a few months after the trial period is over and when we would be able to partake in final negotiations. Then I can put forward the proposal to the Park Authority and then make an effort to amend the contract.

'One important thing to remember is this: there will be enough food for everyone, so don't fight amongst yourselves. And secondly, when we catch prey, all of you—hyenas, vultures, eagles and many other neighbours—are to come to share the food with us. Have we ever said no to you? We never say no to anyone! Willingly or unwillingly, we share food with you all.'

'Mr President, did you invite any of us in the past to share food from you? No, never. You shared food with us as uninvited guests,' came a voice from the crowd.

'Let's move beyond this point and onto what is important here. Once you give names of your family members to the secretary, we can then send this information to the Safari Park Authority, and they can then issue an identity card.

A lot of animals asked, 'What is an identity card? We have never heard speak of such a thing!'

After a short pause, Mr President explained, 'It is a card detailing your name, age and address, and the authority would supply food accordingly. Food will be supplied three times a week—Monday, Wednesday and Saturday.'

'But what happens if we get hungry in between?' someone shouted.

'Where could we hide our food? In the river bank where the hyenas, wild cats and other animals will find and eat it? If we keep our food in the water then other crocodiles will eat our food. We cannot keep an eye on our food at all hours of the day!' said Mr Mamba.

Another argument broke out amongst the hyenas, wild cats and dogs. They all said, in one voice, 'We don't live in the water to rob you! You come to river bank and rob us!'

The arguments were escalating. Mr Simba roared and then pointed to everyone. 'You—all of you!—don't have to keep an eye on your food at all hours of the day! They would get their food from the authority! So why they would steal your food? But, if this hypothetical situation was to arise, if someone is found guilty of stealing food from others, he or she would be severely punished or expelled from the park! The offender may be handed over to the Park Authority to be caged and deported to the zoo for rest of his life, away from his family, friends and relatives.

'Dear friends, let me make it clear to you: we had a tough negotiation with the Park Authority and it was agreed that all adult carnivorous animals, such as big cats, for example—which is defined by those aged three years and older—will get six kilograms of meat every day whilst every child will get four kilograms. Food will be supplied three times a week—Monday, Wednesday and Saturday—from March 1, 2011. So, please send your details to your secretary sooner to get food supplies from March 1, 2011.

Mr Mbwa then asked, 'There are carnivorous animals who do not fall under the category of big cats, so how much food will they get?'

'Less than six kilograms. The Safari Park Authority has got the list of food for each and every animal and will accordingly supply food. If we feel the food supply is not adequate, we will demand more in the future.

Let me just remind you,' he continued, 'it will be illegal to kill any animal in the park from March 1, 2011, and anybody found to be violating the rules will be severely punished. I have already explained to you the nature of punishment so, friends, think ten times before committing any crime.

'Now, are there any more questions? We have had enough discussions in recent weeks. If you need to know more about it this, we can discuss it at our next meeting.'

One sad, worried and bewildered zebra said, in surprise, 'We trust you. We support you and have worked hard for you to achieve your dream. You have got what you wanted—your food supply from the Park Authority—but what we got? We have got nothing. You got your tasty food supplied by the Park Authority but, for us, not even a straw. You used us to get your food.' Many other herbivorous animals showed support for the zebra and shouted against Mr President and the other carnivorous animals.

Mr president, with a smile on his face, replied, 'Be quiet and listen carefully to what I am saying to you. Yes, we got free tasty food from the Safari Park Authority, no doubt about it, but you got the best incomparable deal by supporting us.'

The zebra and many other herbivorous animals laughed and mocked Mr Lion. 'Best deal?' A wave of laughter spread across the herbivorous animals and echoed far into the park.

Mr President then said, 'Do you want to know why we demanded food from the Safari Park Authority? To stop the killing of any innocent creature—creatures like *you*!—for our survival. You got the best deal! Call it *security*!' Mr Simba said in a loud, commanding voice.

The whole park suddenly fell silent for some time.

Mr Simba then said again, 'You can graze anywhere in the park, day and night, without any fear of being eaten by any carnivorous animal. Is that not the best deal for you? Not to mention the fact that your food is in excess in the park!'

The zebra and many other animals apologised.

Nobody asked any more questions that day and Mr Lion closed the opportunity for more discussion, meaning a silence descended, with the meeting declared closed for the day.

Chapter 15:
Signing The Contract

Mr Simba wrote to Mr Thomas mentioning Clause 6 and Clause 7 to be added to the contract for signing. He also confirmed the date for the meeting on February 20, 2011, at the Maasai Mark Park venue, which Mr Thomas accepted.

His team arrived on time and the meeting started.

Mr Thomas said, 'I think we all ought to try hard to sign the contract today.'

Mr Simba and his committee members recognised Mr Thomas did not seem to be in a good mood like in the previous meetings. He looked sad, as if somebody had poured cold water on his face. He was trying to smile, but it was easy to read as artificial, and he also seemed to be quiet and looked worried.

'Are you alright, Mr Thomas?' asked Mr Simba.

'Yes, quiet,' he responded with a smile.

Mr Thomas said to the committee, 'You remember the discussion we had at our last meeting?'

The members all echoed they did.

Mr Simba then informed the committee of the aim for the day's meeting, which was to sign the contract. He then addressed Mr Thomas and asked him to produce the contract.

'I am sorry to inform you, Mr President,' Mr Thomas began, 'that the last two clauses you have proposed are not accepted by us. In Clause 6 you state that the Safari Park Authority cannot kill any Safari Park Animal as a means of supplying food to you or to keep the number of animals under control, but you must understand: if we do not kill animals from the park, where do you think your food supply will come from? Furthermore, if we do not keep the number under control, this park will become over-populated in the future!

'Perhaps you are aware that there are 1.7 million wildebeest and 800,000 gazelle and zebra in the park. Within one year, their number would be 2 million wildebeest and 1 million gazelle and zebra, or maybe more. In this situation, where would you go? Moreover, pasturage would not be enough for the herbivorous animals in the future.'

'We have decided not to kill any animals. They are our brothers and sisters, and we want to live in peace and harmony. How can we watch you kill them in front of us to feed us?' Mr Simba responded.

A lot of the herbivorous animals in the committee felt sad. Miss Pala Hala burst into tears. Even all the carnivorous animals began to feeling uncomfortable upon hearing the news that their brothers and sisters would be killed in front of their eyes for the sake of feeding them.

'The purpose of the movement is all in vain,' Mr Simba said. 'Regarding the control of animals, a lot of them die when trying to cross the river when they go on holiday to the Serengeti Park in Tanzania during October and November, and again when they return from holiday in May and June every year. A lot of them die from diseases and hunger due to a lack of edible grass in the park.

'In addition, we intend to have family planning.'

There was not much room for negotiation. The committee members could not decide on any better option plan to propose to Mr Thomas.

'You have said correctly that there is no edible green grass for the animals and so, within a few years, when their numbers are double, where they will go and what they will eat and, more specifically, where will *you* go?' asked Mr Thomas. 'You have a think on what you would like to do and let me know your decision.

'But what I will say is this: family planning alone will not allow you to be able to effectively control the population, and it will take time to be effective.'

Mr Thomas felt happier for the rest of the meeting. He had managed to restrain the negotiation and create some mistrust amongst animals to stop them from signing the contract. His face became brighter and looked happier. He knew if the contract could not be signed that day, he would be able to buy time and the whole negotiation could very well fall apart. Furthermore, the animals' trust in Mr Simba would be severely dented and passion for the cause would die down.

He then pointed out to Mr president, 'You have decided not to kill any animals and to instead live in peace and harmony, which is an excellent idea that we all support. But if anybody from outside the park comes and kills any animals, how can you stop this? You are a non-violent community. And then consider, when the news spreads to outside the park, poachers will be attracted and you will be killed in large numbers for various reasons. How are you going to protect yourselves?'

'You have raised a very valid point,' Mr Simba responded. 'We are a peace-loving community; however, that does not mean we are weak and cannot and will not protect ourselves. Together we all will protect our homeland and ourselves and our neighbours. Anybody that tries to create any rift amongst us or any invader to our land will be severely punished. In future, he will not dare think of harming us.'

You also have Safari Park guards to protect the park from poachers... Isn't that the case, Mr Thomas?'

'Yes.'

Mr Simba realised he was in deep trouble. He had promised everybody they would get free food from the Safari Park Authority and there would be no killing in the park; now, however, the negotiation seemed to be at a stake.

He knew he had to find some alternate solution to maintain his face and the cause.

'I still feel we will find some solution,' Mr O'Ginga interjected.

Mr Amolo murmured to his colleague Mr O'Dinga, 'I don't think we're going to be as lucky as we thought in achieving our demands of the Safari Park Authority.'

Mr O'Dinga said, 'We need to think about other alternatives. We need some more time. Now, let us move on to Clause 7.'

'Of course you would be informed if or when we take any major decisions to do any work in the park,' Mr Thomas said.

Mr Simba then asked for a few minutes to discuss Clause 6 with his committee members.

Mr Thomas, accompanied by his committee members, left the place, escorted by Kifaru to the safari jeep.

Mr Simba discussed with his committee members how the problem could be resolved. Various committee members put forward their opinions, but time was running out and no proposal was accepted by all the animal groups.

Mr O'Dinga suggested, 'If the Safari Park Authorit removes a few old infirm, terminally ill animals or carcass from the park, we should not object. It will keep the animal numbers under control.'

In conclusion, it was decided that, yes, this was the best proposal. They were able to remove a few old and infirm animals from the park—not in the daylight but in the dark, without any body's notice, in order to keep the number under control.

Mr Thomas and his colleagues soon returned and the meeting started again.

Mr Simba informed Mr Thomas of the committee members; decision regarding Clause 6, and stated that they would have the power to remove carcasses, and old and infirm and terminally ill animals from the park from time to time, but to do so only in the dark.

Clause 7 remained unchanged.

The contract was then signed between the Maasai Mara Residents Association and the Maasai Mara Safari Park authority on February 22, 2011 for implementation from March 1, 2011.

Mr Simba thanked Mr Thomas, holding out his paw and shaking Mr Thomas's hand. It was a very happy occasion; everybody felt great relief from the tiring few months and painstaking hard work.

At that very moment, Mr Simba was about to roar but, with great difficulty, he held his tongue: he realised he is in a meeting and should act as the president of the organisation and should not behave like an animal. If he was to behave like an animal, what his committee members think of him?

After the meeting was over, Mr Simba asked Mr O'Dingo, Mr Tembo and various other committee members to escort Mr Thomas and his team to the safari jeep, which was waiting nearby. He asked all committee members to wait. Having escorted the delegates, Mr Tembo and the other committee members went to see Mr Thomas and then returned.

Mr Simba then addressed everyone. 'Dear friends, I am very happy that, at last, a deal has been achieved. We will all have food supplied by the Park Authority. We need to inform the general members about the deal and plan how to organise ourselves when the food supply comes in.

He then turned his attention to the eagle and asked that he inform all the residents of the Maasai Mara Park, including the Maasai people, to attend a meeting on February 24, 2011, at 1PM in their usual venue beside the River Mara. He said, 'Till that day, committee members should not disclose the deal to anyone, not even to family members. I do not want this news to leak. Time is very short and so I will request you to spread the invitation this afternoon before the safari jeeps come to the park.'

Mr Duma said, 'This is good news and I don't see any reason to hide it! I cannot stop hiding this good news for long. I am trembling inside with the sheer joy of it!'

Mr Simba said, 'Sometimes you have to control your emotions and instincts. In just two days we will inform everybody of the good news. If you inform your friends then many animals will question why they were not informed about this. That will create distrust amongst us. I am sure you all are tired so go home and take rest. I will see you on Thursday.'

Mr Simba could hardly believe he had achieved what he wanted. He went home happily and told his wives that he would like to spend two days with the family in their holiday den, and so they were to get ready. They asked whether the meeting had been a success, to which Mr Simba replied 'I am very happy. On Thursday I will announce the results to the public.'

CHAPTER 16:
VICTORY FOR THE ASSOCIATION

At last, the day arrived for the meeting.

As always, the meeting started on time under the familiar umbrella acacia tree. The whole area was packed with animals, and the trees were packed with birds, with the eagles hovering over the venue and vultures sitting atop the strong trees. Many other birds—whom nobody had ever seen before—were also visible at the meeting.

The curious Maasai people had also attended, accompanied by their leader.

Mr Simba, leader of the Animals Association, addressed the crowd. 'Dear friends, sisters and brothers, today we have some happy news for you.'

Everybody shouted in one voice, 'Yes! Yes!'

After a long struggle lasting five months, and thanks to your sacrifice, your determination, and your cooperation, we have achieved what has been long deserved for us. We have got what we wanted. Now it is your duty to maintain what we have achieved.'

Everybody shouted again. 'Yes! Yes!'

We have signed a contract with the Maasai Mara Safari Park Authority, applied from March 1, 2011. Our food will be supplied by The Safari Park Authority. Now, we will no longer kill any innocent, helpless or weak animals or men. We will not kill or harm those who cannot protect themselves. We have had enough bloodshed in this park in the past—but now there will be no more! There will be no bloodshed in this park in the future. It is illegal to kill any animal or to harm anybody on or after March 1, 2011.'

Once again, everybody shouted in one voice. 'Yes! Yes!'

'The Maasai people are our friends and neighbours. They can come to this park at any time, whenever they want. They can graze their animals in the park anytime they like, without any fear of being attacked by any animal. We can go there without any fear of being attacked by the Maasai people.

'I will request of you that, if you haven't submitted your name, den, track number and number of family members to our accountant, please do hurry and do so if you want to get your food supplied by the Authority on March 1, 2011. Failure to do so will mean you will not get your food from the authority.'

Mr Simba then informed the crowd, that, 'This day will be celebrated as Liberation Day for the residents of the Maasai Mara Park! We will organise an entertainment programme, such as melodious song by various birds, dances by various groups of animal and a variety of other activities. The Maasai people will show their colourful dance. Please submit your name to our General Secretary if you would like to participate in the programme.'

Nobody in the park could sleep that night. Mr Lion was the same, with an immensely complex thought tormenting his brain, traveling from one cell to another. Everybody was excited but Mr Simba, having various thoughts in his mind, was far from able to relax. He thought of what if the food supply did not arrive in time and how the animals would react. He was glad some of his supporters, particularly Mr O'Dingo, were also confident that the food supply would come.

The following morning, many animals assembled in the designated area where the food was to be served. There was a long queue of various carnivorous animals, all waiting for food. The herbivorous animals were also present just to watch what would happen.

The food was scheduled to arrive at midday, but no cars were seen in the vicinity.

One carnivorous animal said loudly to the president, 'I know this was a conspiracy to decisive us!' He was being vindictive and had a negative attitude towards the president because of the delay in the food supply. As a result, he was severely scolded by many other carnivorous animals, and so he shut his mouth immediately.

'Of course the food will come very soon,' said the Maasai leader.

Some herbivorous animals asked their friends to go into hiding. 'Hungry carnivorous animals are dangerous,' they recognised. 'You cannot trust them at all. And now their food supply is not coming...'

'Why are we wasting our time standing in-front of hungry, brutal animals, dressed like snacks on a plate?' asked one. 'We are their enemy! We are also hungry so let's go grazing.'

Many of the herbivorous animals made the decision to leave the place. Some of the carnivorous animals were becoming restless and impatient.

Suddenly, one of the animals spotted a safari cars heading towards them and shouted for joy, 'The food is coming! The food is coming!'

The food supply was now one hour late. All the carnivorous animals were very hungry as they had not killed any animals the previous evening, thinking their food supply would arrive on time for their lunch at around 12 noon. Some of the animals were very agitated and verbally abusive towards their president, whereas others were suspicious.

'Is this some kind of plan?'

'Surely not. Mr Thomas is not the kind of person to deceive. There must be some other reason for the delay. Mr Thomas knows very well of the consequences if he tries to deceive us.'

Mr Simba discussed with the Maasai leader that he was confident the food would come—and very soon. 'There may be some problem with the transportation or the people might be frightened to come here to distribute food to us. When they come, please try to be polite to them and never show any aggression. Do not frighten them. Try to be friendly with them. They will be armed so do not get frightened upon seeing the guns or armed guards.'

Mr Twiga, the tallest animal in the park, saw some jeeps approaching the park. He shouted with joy, 'They are coming! They are coming!' The eagle and vulture flew to inspect who was coming to the park. In no time, they scanned the whole park and confirmed it was their food supply cars. Everybody waited eagerly.

'Mr Thomas said, with a smile on his face, 'I am sorry, Mr President, that we are late.' Looking in the eyes of Mr Simba, he continued, 'I am sure everybody is very hungry.'

Mr Simba shrugged his neck, lifted his paw and stretched it out to Mr Thomas. 'Certainly. You will be surprised to know that nobody killed any animals last night owing to the fact they will satisfy their stomachs fully today.'

'The people are scared to come here,' Mr Thomas explained. 'A lot of them threatened me that they will leave their job if they are forced to distribute food to the animals in an open field. Of course, I assured them that there is no reason for them to be scared and that I, too, would be in attendance. I further reiterated that Mr Simba is a very polite and honest lion and that he will not deceive us!'

Mr Simba welcomed all the people who had come to distribute the food and said, 'In future, you should not be scared of us. We are harmless to our friends and to any other creatures in this world. However, this does not mean we are weak. We are ferocious. If anybody tries to attack us or our homeland, we know how to protect ourselves.

'I know you are very hungry, so please be patient,' he continued to the animals.

People were unloading food from the car. Mr Simba asked the committee members to help to distribute the food once it was ready for distribution. 'Please come one by one and tell the committee members your den number, track name and the number of adults and children living in the den. The committee members will help you if any problems arise.'

Mr Simba, Mr Thomas and Mr O'Dingo went to one side and started talking amongst themselves whilst keeping an eye on the activities. Mr O'Dinga then said, 'Isn't this unique? This situation was unthinkable months ago but now it has become a reality.'

'Indeed,' Mr Thomas replied in a surprised tone. 'I would never have imagined it. I was concerned how the food was being distributed to hungry carnivorous animals.'

It took an hour to distribution the food, without any incident. Moreover, there was some surplus food, meaning the eagles and vultures got their share of food separately, without sharing the food of other animals. They wanted their food from the Safari Park Authority and did not want to share food from other carnivorous animals. They were very happy to have their own food from the authority as they got recognition as a part of the animal kingdom.

Mr Thomas thanked Mr Simba and said, 'I am grateful to you. It was a very well planned, disciplined approach. I am sure in the future it will continue like this.'

Mr President thanked Mr Thomas and all the food distributing team. He said, 'Dear friends, the next food supply will be in two days' time on Thursday. Please note that food supplies are every Tuesday, Thursday and Saturday at 12 noon, here in this place.' He glanced around to see if the animals were enjoying their food and was satisfied that everybody was enjoying their food in peace.

The Safari Park Authority left the park at around half-past two in the afternoon.

'Dear friends, please take some rest. We will start our entertainment programme at 6.30PM after all the safari jeeps leave the park,' said Mr Simba. 'Mr Tembo will inform you about the programme.'

After lunch, everybody felt very full and sleepy. All the animals lay down on the grass. Some started gossiping whilst some animals fell asleep in no time and started snoring. Nearby, the babies of the lions, elephants, deer and others played together. Clouds gathered in the sky, giving some shade to those who were sleeping in the scorching heat.

Mr Simba's eager eyes were searching for the infirm hungry leopard who had come to him for help. He asked Mr Tembo and the other animals who were present in the meeting on that day, but everybody replied that they had not seen him.

Mr Simba's joy turn to anguish. He sent one leopard and an elephant to the infirm leopard's den with some food and was eagerly waiting to know what had happened to him. He had hoped they would come with good news that the leopard was alive and in good health.

The entertainment programme started in time once the last safari park jeep had left the park.

Mr President gave a speech. 'Dear friends, sisters and brothers of the Maasai Mara...'

There was a big applause for Mr Simba.

'How are you all doing?'

Everybody cheered.

'Did you eat fully? Was the food good?' The lion's voice echoed across the park like before.

Everybody shouted in unison, 'Yes! The food was very good and enough for everybody to eat until their stomachs were full! We enjoyed it thoroughly—and thank you for all that you have done for us!'

'After the hard work the last five months,' Mr Simba continued, 'I am delighted to see our dream has come true. And from today, killing any creature of God is illegal in the Maasai Mara and outside the park, including the Maasai people who live just outside the park. They can come with their herds any time for grazing. They are also a part of our society. They have got the birth-right in this park, as you have got. As we discussed in the past, anybody found guilty of theft, or of causing harm or injury to others, will be severely punished or may even be expelled from the park depending on their crime. So, friends, before you commit any crime, think consequences. I am confident no such incident will happen. So with that said, please enjoy this evening throughout the night without any fear. I will request that Mr Tembo start the programme.'

Mr Tembo raised his trunk and said, 'Dear friends, we are going to start the programme! Please take you seats. Our first performer is Lilac

Breasted rollers. He does not need any introduction. You must have seen his dance. Today he will show his special dance from the sky!'

The Lilac Breasted Roller swooped around the sky for some time and entertained the crowd. Everybody watched his dance and enjoyed it thoroughly.

When the dance ended, Mr Tembo asked, 'Was it not a fantastic dance? I have never seen anything like that before!

'Now, our next performer is the long-tailed Jackson's Widow Bird, who will show his dancing talent on the ground. I am sure some of you have seen his dance before.'

The Jackson's Widow Bird entertained everybody on the ground with his excellent performance. Everybody applauded. The crowd shouted, 'Encore! Encore!'

Mr Tembo announced, 'Our next performers are a group of colourful Superb Starlings, who will sing a carouse song.'

The entertainment continued into the night, with the Red-Wattled Lapwing performing a dance from the sky, a Gray-Crowned Crane dancing a colourful dance, and the newly formed Tana Dance Group consisting of animals, birds, antelope and others providing a dance and song. There was long applaud for the dance group; they performed for a full half an hour, but still there was a request to continue the dance.

Mr Tembo said, 'Don't worry, my friends, they will perform again in the near future. This is just beginning of the plan!'

The entertainment programme was ongoing until past midnight. It seemed that nobody wanted to go home—and now there was no necessity to go home. The whole Maasai Mara Park was now everybody's home, and they all wanted to enjoy each and every moment of it. Some animals slept where they were watching the programme, and did so without any fear, which would have been an unthinkable suggested a few months before.

When they woke the next morning, they saw a New Dawn, a New World, with the Maasai Mara Safari Park safer than any civilised cities in the world at night or day.

All the residents were proud of that—and proud they should be.

THE END

ABOUT THE AUTHOR

Author Dr Somendra Lal Ghose was born in Dibrugarh Assam India. He qualified as a doctor (Bachelor of Medicine and Bachelor of Surgery) in 1970 and came to Delhi to pursue higher studies. He achieved a Master's degree in Orthopaedic from the All India Institute of Medical Sciences, New Delhi, in 1975, and worked there for a year before leaving for the UK. He worked in Orthopaedics in various hospitals in the UK. Finally, he decided to become a general practitioner and so, since 1986, has been working as a General Practitioner in Liverpool.

Dr Ghose has many hobbies. He loves writing, cooking, gardening and travelling. He has written a few books in Bengali, including a poetry book. In his spare time, he enjoys painting and also likes to travel. He continues to work as a part-time General Practitioner whilst the rest of the time directs his attention to his hobbies.

He was General Secretary of Bengali Association in Merseyside for six years and then

Vice President for six years. He believes in living a very simple life. He is well known and respected in the community.

Somendra visited the Maasai Mara Safari Park and other safari parks in Kenya in October 2010. Upon returning from Kenya, he started writing this short fantasy story. He had a clear idea what he wanted to write. He finished writing in six months.

ANIMALS IN MAASAI LANGUAGE

Buffalo (Nyati):	One of the big five animals
Cheetah (Duma):	Runs very fast to catch its prey but only a short distance.
Crocodile (Mamba):	Can grow to be 7 metres long.
Dik Dik (Dik dik):	They make a noises *dik dik*, and are the smallest antelopes.
Eagle (Tai):	A large bird of prey.
Elephant (Tembo/Ndovu):	One of the big fives. The largest and heaviest herbivorous animal. A large number are seen in Maasai Mara Park.
Fox (Mbweha)	
Gazelle (Swala):	These and zebra numbers are roughly 800,000.
Giraffe (Twiga):	The tallest animal.
Hippopotamus (Kiboko)	
Hyena (Fisi):	A scavenging animal that moves in groups.

Impala (Swala Pala):	Common antelope; good jumper.
Lion (Simba):	One of the big fives. Moves in groups. Most of the time, takes rest. Eats approximately 7kg meat every day. Lionesses eat approximately 5kg meat a day. Rests approximately 20 hours a day.
Leopard (Chui):	One of big fives. Expert in climbing trees. Hides food in the trees.
Monkey (Nyani)	
Rhinoceros (Kifaru):	One of big five. Poor eye sight, good sense of smell.
Roan Antelope (Korongo)	
Sable Antelope (Pala hala)	
Wildebeest (Nyumbu):	Mass migratory animal from Maasai Mara to Serengeti. Numbers amounting to 1.7 million.
Zebra (Punda Milia):	Is the size of a donkey but striped; each stripe is different and so acts like a human fingerprint.
Wild Dog (Mbwa)	

ACKNOWLEDGEMENTS

I am grateful to all those well-wishers who have helped me in many different ways when it came to writing this; offering their support by reading the manuscript and expressing their sincere opinion and encouraging me to pursue publication.

I don't want to mention any names and disappoint those whose names are not mentioned.

CPSIA information can be obtained
at www.ICGtesting.com
Printed in the USA
BVHW060820030719
552582BV00026B/1153/P